JOURNAL FOR THE STUDY OF
SUPPLEMENT

5

Editors

Ernst Bam

Anthony Ha

David H

Max Wil

Executive

Bruce D C

Department of Bi
The University
Sheffield S
Engla

THE
PEOPLE
OF
GOD

MARKUS BARTH

Journal for the Study of the New Testament
Supplement Series, 5

Sheffield

1983

Published by
JSOT Press
Department of Biblical Studies
The University of Sheffield
Sheffield S10 2TN
England

Printed in Great Britain
by Redwood Burn Ltd.
Trowbridge, Wiltshire.

British Library Cataloguing in Publication Data

Barth, Markus
    The People of God.—(Journal for the Study of the New
    Testament Supplement series, ISSN 0143-5108; 5)
    1. Bible. N.T. Epistles of Paul
    2. Palestine in Judaism
    I. Title   II. Series
    296.3'87   BS2655.J4

    ISBN 0-905774 54 X
    ISBN 0-905774 55 8 PbK

CONTENTS

Preface   7

Introduction   9

I Tensions in Paul and among his Interpreters   11

II The Testimony of Romans 9-11 and other
   Pauline Texts   29

III The Church and the Jewish People Today   51

Notes   73

Index of Passage References   95
Index of Names   99
Index of Documents   101

PREFACE

This book has its origin in a series of lectures delivered before both expert and lay audiences. The occasions for the addresses were provided, first, by a conference of Jews and Christians (held in the Katholische Akademie in Munich early in 1976) brought together to consider the topic 'Paul—Apostat oder Apostel?', and, secondly, by a lectureship to which the Principal of Westminster College, Cambridge, invited me in January 1977. Discussion at the two venues, further study and consequent revision of the lectures have resulted in the written form here published: an earlier version, in German, was made available in *Paulus—Apostat oder Apostel?* (Regensburg: Pustet, 1977) 45-124. I also wish to express my thanks and admiration here to Dr. David Hill of the Department of Biblical Studies, Sheffield University, for the excellent work he did in transforming my English text into a clear and fluent English.

Historical information, biblical interpretation, reflections in the area of dogmatics and urgent recommendations to take a stand on vital, contemporary issues are all combined in the following pages. Because unity in matters of faith depends upon truth, and because brotherly conduct in daily life is based on faithfulness, it has been necessary to go back once more to the biblical evidence, to assess critically the major (and some minor) currents in both the Jewish and Christian usage of Scripture, and to issue a plea for honest repentance and courageous action.

It makes no sense to confine theological activity to an ivory tower. The importance of the search for the 'People of God' may be gauged by its relevance to at least four issues confronting us at the present time:

the baffling fate and often shocking politics of the State of Israel since the Six Day War in 1967;

the anti-Jewish sentiments which still disgrace many books written for the church and many declarations made about the church;

the faltering progress which characterizes endeavours towards ecumenical unity;

finally, the need for a united and unequivocal testimony to Jesus, a Jew and God's son, and, as such, the saviour of the world.

If the chapters which follow together assist the search for a solution to these or other similarly profound problems, this small book will have fulfilled its purpose.

Markus Barth
Basel, March 31, 1982

INTRODUCTION

Who are the people of God? Jews, Christians, both together, or neither of them? Pope John XXIII showed a way to answer this question when in October 1960 he received in audience a group of American Jews and greeted them with the words, 'Son io Giuseppe, il fratello vostro (I am Joseph, your brother).' By this allusion to the story of Joseph and his brothers (Gen. 45:4) he revealed how deeply he was affected by the distress and anguish of persecuted Jews, and how serious was his intention to establish the closest possible relationship between Jews and Christians.

Twenty-two years earlier Pope Pius XI had designated Christians as 'spiritual Semites,' but John XXIII surpassed his predecessor not merely by the warmth of his diction: his greeting hinted at the unique and specific brotherhood uniting Jews and Christians. The kind of brotherly feelings which every decent human being ought to have for every fellow human creature can never exhaust what Pope John had in mind. Rather he was describing Jews and Christians as members of the same family and a people which is constituted and kept alive as a very special group among all tribes and nations.

'Christians and Jews are truly brothers in faith.' Implicitly the Pope abandoned the monopoly claim by some Christians on the title 'people of God'. In the house of the common Father no more than the modest place of the younger brother—and among the people of God only the position of a newcomer—can be occupied by the Gentile Christians who form the vast majority in the Catholic, the Protestant and the Free Churches.

In the Roman Catholic Church the right word spoken at the right time by a warm-hearted man had the effect of a first rain-shower after a period of drought. It brought about first the revision of liturgical texts which had been insulting to Jewish hearers and prone to keep anti-Judaism alive among Christians; it stimulated the preparation and proclamation of *Nostra Aetate* (chapter IV) within the framework of the Second Vatican Council; in April 1973 it led to the publication of a *Pastoral Admonition* by the French Bishops, and in January 1975 to the issue of the *Orientations et Suggestions* from the Vatican Secretariat for Christian Unity. Before, with, and after the steps taken in Roman Catholic quarters, a host of church declarations and private studies appeared in the Netherlands, in Geneva, in Germany and elsewhere.[1] The movement has not yet stopped, and it deserves to be welcomed and encouraged by all who are ready to ask, What does it mean to be a Christian and to be counted a member of God's people?

In the following three chapters, I intend first to deal with *problems* posed by the apostle Paul's utterances on the people of God (Chapter One), then with the *arguments* he uses to establish the oneness and unity of this people (Chapter Two), and finally with *consequences* of his teaching for the common life of Jews and Christians at the present time (Chapter Three).

Chapter One

TENSIONS IN PAUL AND AMONG HIS INTERPRETERS

In what way and with what restrictions and specifications does Paul speak about the people of God, and how have his elaborations on this theme been understood?

A. Israel's Titles for the Church

When Paul speaks of the church, he has in mind the community worshipping God, the Father of Jesus Christ. The church universal is visibly manifested either in local congregations or in house churches. Most frequently the apostle designates the church by the noun ἐκκλησία; sometimes, however, he also uses the term λαός (from which 'laity' is derived). λαός is in the Old Testament (LXX) an honorific title, normally employed in the singular as a description of the people of Israel.[1] In the Pauline writings, just as in letters written under Paul's influence, such as Titus (2:14) and I Peter (2:9-10), λαός appears either when the Old Testament is quoted or in contexts which contain intended allusions to the terminology and history of Israel. While at times the term designates the Jewish people before the advent of Jesus Christ,[2] in Rom. 9:25-26, I Cor. 14:21 and II Cor. 6:16, λαός refers to the whole of Christianity, the community of those called from Jews and from Gentiles.

On the other hand, when groups of Christians or the whole of Christianity are called ἐκκλησία,[3] a term is being used which among Greek-speaking people denoted the 'assembly' in which citizens of Hellenistic towns exerted their political rights and fulfilled their public responsibility.[4] The church is distinct from those assemblies because it is called together and constituted *by God*; its members are the citizens of heaven (Phil. 3:20; Eph. 2:19);[5] it is the congregation of sons come of age to whom a royal responsibility is entrusted by God himself[6]—it includes not only sons, but also daughters, not only freemen, but also slaves. Even more important than the analogy between the church and the hellenistic town-assemblies is the connection between the ἐκκλησία of the New Testament and the Old Testament קָהָל or עֵדָה of Yahweh,[7] i.e. an assembly of the people of

Israel such as that at Shechem (Josh. 24) which at one and the same time had religious, cultural, legal and political character. Paul seldom spoke of the church without using a terminology that alludes to the life, history, and language of Israel.

The question must be asked: Is the people of God in its New Testament form the competitor, successor or partner of the elect people, the Jews? Or, on the other hand, should Paul be regarded as having thought in terms of a unilateral dependence which might include an indissoluble identity?

Identity in dependence is supported by a series of collective and individual predicates which depict the church and her members as participants in the rights and tasks of Israel. *Collective* Israelite names or descriptions are used when Paul denotes the church as the 'bride' (of Christ) in II Cor. 11:2, Eph. 5:25-27;[8] as the 'temple of God' in I Cor. 3:16 and Eph. 2:20-22; or as 'the circumcision' in Phil. 3:3. Some Old Testament and Jewish honorific titles are not transferred to the church as a whole but are reserved either for Jesus Christ alone, or for him and the individual members of the congregation. 'Son of God,' 'only-begotten,' 'beloved,' 'chosen,' 'seed of Abraham,' 'servant,' belong in this category. Instead of calling those people 'Christians' who confess that 'Jesus Christ is Lord,' Paul speaks of them as 'sons of God' (Gal. 3:26; Rom. 8:14, 19), 'children of Abraham' (Gal. 3:7, 29), 'God's chosen ones' (Rom. 8:33; cf. Col. 3:12; II Tim. 2:10; Tit. 1:1), 'saints' (*passim*). He describes them as branches grafted into the holy root (Rom. 11:16ff.), members of the new covenant (Gal. 4:24-31; I Cor. 11:25; II Cor. 3:4-18), children of the heavenly Jerusalem (Gal. 4:26). These members of the church celebrate and eat the Paschal meal provided by God (I Cor. 5:7-8); they bear resemblance to the Exodus community in the temptation they experience and in the protection granted them by God (I Cor. 10:1-13). What is true of Old Testament priests and sacrifices applies to them as well (I Cor. 10:18-21; Rom. 12:1-2). The body of each Christian is called a 'temple' (I Cor. 6:19).

The transference of collective titles of Israel to *individual* members of the people had been prepared for in the Old Testament itself. In the historical books and in the collection of prophetic writings, in hymns and prayers, Abraham, David, and other members of the people chosen for specific tasks are depicted as representatives of each pious individual. Ezek. 18, with its emphasis upon the accountability of each single person, is an early landmark in this development. Finally, in Jewish Wisdom literature as well as in Philo and in apocalyptic and rabbinical writings more and more emphasis is placed on the attitude of each individual.

Does this mean that according to Paul also the *individual* person who has decided to believe in Christ has replaced the *community* of the people of God who lived in and with and from the faith of the Fathers? If that were so, no longer would a people as a whole be the chosen covenant partner of God. Rather, the terms 'people' and 'assembly' (λαός and ἐκκλησία) would signify no more than the gathering or the sum-total of individual members, each one of them approached by God and having access to him in his own way.

This conclusion is prohibited by all that Paul affirms about Christ and Adam in I Cor. 15 and Rom. 5, about 'our father Abraham' in Gal. 3 and Rom. 4, and about the continued close relationship between, on the one hand, God, Christ, Paul, and Gentile-Christian churches and, on the other, Israel, Jews and Jerusalem (cf. Gal. 1-2, 4; II Cor. 3; Rom. 9-11; Phil. 3; and all passages dealing with the collection for Jerusalem). In the First and Last Man, in Adam and in Christ, all mankind is included and forms a community, not just an agglomeration of sinners who are redeemed. One patriarch represents the community of all who believe, be they Jews or Gentiles by origin. One apostle's service fulfils the new dispensation and covenant which unites Jews and Gentiles under the same grace of God. The collection organised in all the major churches founded by Paul is a testimony to dependence upon and gratitude for Jerusalem (see esp. II Cor. 8-9). Thus in the Pauline writings the Old Testament and Jewish corporate thinking concerning creation, election, sin, salvation, faith and obedience has simply not been relinquished or abolished in favour of radical or total individualization.[9]

There is, however, one individual person whose function cannot be emphasized strongly enough: it is the person of The Man, Jesus Christ, the head of his body, the Messiah of Israel. While the individuality of the church members does not hold a determining position like that of Jesus Christ, Paul does recognize that the Holy Spirit creates and moves single members of the church in special ways and gives them functions of honour within the whole of God's people. Since our present subject is the people of God rather than the personal ministries within that people, contributions of individual members to the common life of God's people will be mentioned only marginally.

Collective and individual titles stemming from Israel and attributed to the church are found not only in Paul's writings. In I Peter (2:4-10) a whole catalogue of them is brought together: holy, royal priesthood, chosen race, holy nation, God's own people, etc. Other parts of the New Testament describe the church in such ways as the people of the Twelve Tribes (Matt. 19:28; Jas. 1:1; Rev. 7:4ff.; 21:12) and as the community of the Exodus (Rev. 15). It was not an original idea of Paul to emphasize the special relationship between Israel and the church; he was probably following an early tradition of preaching, teaching, or praying when he called the church and/or the Jewish people the 'Israel of God' in Gal. 6:16 and when he spoke of 'all Israel' in Rom. 11:26.

Even within Judaism some of Israel's titles were selected and used to describe reformed or newly constituted congregations. Already before Paul's time the Rechabites, the Hasidim, the Therapeutae, the Qumran Community and other baptising groups considered themselves, with modesty or with great pride, as the 'remnant' of the holy people.[10] But, unlike the apostle Paul, they appear not to have believed in the future salvation of the totality of Israel, and they did not think of the admission of Gentiles in large numbers to God's holy people; only individual Gentiles who were willing to subject themselves to the whole Law could acquire the status of full Jews.

Paul, however, upholds the claim and promise of God concerning 'all Israel' even when he speaks of the 'remnant,' and he combines—as will be shown later—the ideas of a remnant, of the whole of Israel, and of the 'full number of the Gentiles' in a unique way (Rom. 9:29; 10:18-21; 11:25-32). According to the apostle the dividing wall between those who were far off and those who were near was torn down. When in Christ's death and resurrection the Law was fulfilled, then peace was also made between the former enemies, and a new man was created, made up of Jews and Gentiles (Gal. 2:18; 3:28; Eph. 2:11-18). In the church neither circumcision nor uncircumcision counts for anything, but rather the keeping of the commandments, faith working through love, and the new creation (I Cor. 7:19; Gal. 5:6; 6:15). Since the church is one single people in which there can no longer be any division between Jews and Gentiles, a sharp separation of Jews from the church seems impossible.

The documents emerging from *western* churches and scholars involved in the issue (mentioned in note 1 to the Introduction) place much emphasis on the stability of God's election and covenant. A few voices seem willing to affirm that the term 'new covenant' (or 'New Testament') connotes the renewal, confirmation, and fulfilment of the ('old') covenant made with the Patriarchs, David, and the whole of Israel—rather than the abolition and negation of the promises made of old by God.[11] Paul could and did speak of the indestructible love of God for the Jewish people 'for the sake of the fathers,' and the apostle's own faithfulness to his 'brethren according to the flesh' ought not to be questioned (Rom. 9:1-6a; 11:28-29). This man characterised as 'a transgressor of God's Law' anyone who would try to rebuild the broken wall of division that once stood between the people of the old and the new covenants (Eph. 2:14; Gal. 2:14-21).

B. The Church Opposed to Israel

Unanswered as yet is the question whether or not of all people the apostle Paul is responsible for the sharp division and final break between Jews and Christians.

Whereas in recent decades Jewish books about Jesus have step-by-step reclaimed Jesus of Nazareth as a good Jewish prophet,[12] the verdict on the apostle Paul, which judges him a disloyal member of his people, still survives. He was declared an apostate in the twelfth Benediction of the Eighteen Petitions Prayer (the שמני עשרי) and has been considered a prodigal son among Jews ever since — though some notable exceptions will have to be mentioned later. The Jewish-Christian *Pseudo-Clementines* represent him as a visionary and magician, inspired by demons, one who had no communion with Jesus and was in disagreement with Jesus' fulfilment of the Law.[13] The schismatic, if not destructive, function of Paul over against Israel was affirmed and consolidated in the interpretations of Marcion and Augustine, Luther and the Tübingen school, and it reverberates still in the theology of R. Bultmann and E. Käsemann.[14]

Indeed, a series of passages and whole contexts can be invoked where Paul, as much as Jesus, draws clear demarcation lines between Jews and Christians. Since both argue in sharp terms explicitly *against* Jews, they appear to be declaring that Jews are separated from God's people.

According to the Gospels Jesus did threaten the sons of the kingdom with expulsion: they will be 'thrown out' (Matt. 8:11f.; Luke 13:28). He did curse the barren fig tree (Matt. 21:18f.); he reproached the Pharisees for not knowing the hour (Luke 19:44); he predicted the destruction of Jerusalem and of the temple because God's people had murdered its prophets (Matt. 23:37; 24:2; 26:61 par.). The Jews were to be smashed by the same cornerstone at which they had taken offence. God's vineyard was to be given to another people (Luke 20:15-18 par.). According to John 8:44, Jesus called certain Judaeans 'children of the devil.' The book of Acts contains accounts of the sermons of Peter and John in which the Jews are branded as murderers of Jesus Christ.[15]

It is not certain whether, after Stephen (Acts 7), Paul was the first Christian to put together (in I Thess. 2.15-16) a catalogue of Jewish misdeeds and their consequences. The apostle charges the Jews with murder of Jesus and the prophets, persecution of the apostles, giving displeasure to God and opposing all men, impeding the preaching of salvation among the Gentiles—all with the effect of filling up the measure of their sins and calling upon themselves the wrath of God until the end of time. In Gal. 4:29-30 the apostle reminds the readers that the slave (Hagar) and her son (Ishmael) were 'thrown out.' The originally noble branches of the olive tree were 'not spared' but 'broken off' (Rom. 11:19-21). According to Paul, God's chosen people was unfaithful. The apostle appears to generalise in a malicious way when he speaks of the absence of righteousness, knowledge and obedience from (the whole of) 'Israel' or 'all' (Israelites).[16] But in the same breath he asserts that God's faithfulness remains unshaken and cannot be abrogated. He gives evidence of an unbroken relationship when he states that only 'some' or 'a part' of God's chosen people were unfaithful, while by the grace of God a 'remnant' (of obedient and faithful people) was left.[17] Paul's harsh judgements on Israel's failure are further mitigated or defused when he attributes the rejection of the Messiah Jesus to a hardening effected by God[18] and to an attitude caused by ignorance.[19]

On which of these seemingly contradictory utterances shall we rely? To this day many Christians (among them especially the leaders of middle eastern churches, but also some prominent western theologians) read Paul as though he had excluded for the present time the possibility of a brotherly relation between Israel and the church.[20] They believe that they are being faithful to Paul when (admittedly under the influence of the political and social consequences of the foundation of the state of Israel) they proclaim: Israel, the Jews, do not belong any more to the people of God! Thrown out of God's covenant as they are, they must be considered a nation like other nations and treated like any pagan people.[21] These Christians understand the concept 'New Covenant' in the sense of a complete abrogation of the Old; therefore they deny the continued validity of Israel's particular election and of the promise of the land to the children of Jacob. The distinctions made between Old and New Covenant (in II Cor. 3; Gal. 4:21-31; see also Heb. *passim*, esp. 8:13) induce them to regard the New Covenant, though it fulfils ancient promises, as something altogether different: it replaces and invalidates the Old. Because of the difference between the Old and the New *Covenants* they also differentiate between an old and a new, a preliminary and a final, a fleshly and a spiritual, a false and a true *people* of God. Indeed, almost everywhere, the church likes to consider herself as the new and true people of God, even at the expense of the Jews.

However, not only in middle eastern churches and not only in reaction to modern Zionism is the distinction or separation made between two different peoples of God of whom the second supersedes the first. None of the canonical Gospels gives its testimony to Christ without making reference to the resistance to Jesus on the part of the Pharisees and the Sanhedrin under its Sadducean leadership. Matthew's version of the Sermon on the Mount is directed to a large extent at a Jewish opposition—be it Pharisaical-rabbinic, Zealotic or Qumranic. Paul's doctrine of the grace and righteousness of God includes a refutation of the belief that by human merits and righteousness the Law can be fulfilled. He found and fought this belief among both Jews and Judaizing Christians,[22] and he appears to reject totally—together with the practice of circumcision (which his opponents prescribed for Christians in Jerusalem, Antioch, Galatia, Rome, Philippi (and Colossae?)—the circumcised people.[23]

Thus it seems that the glorious extension of the titles describing Israel's privileges and their application to the community of Jews and Gentiles is counteracted by a disparaging limitation of the same titles: 'Not all of Israel are Israel' (Rom. 9:6). At the same time when God's promise to Israel is fulfilled in historic events, the chosen people is reduced to a mere remnant.[24] Indeed, judgement and division were foreshadowed already at the beginning and during the course of Israel's history, as shown by the contrasts between Jacob and Esau, Isaac and Ishmael, the faithful Abraham and the slavish subjects of the Law, the heavenly and the present Jerusalem, useful and useless vessels, a rejected majority and a holy remnant.[25] How *could* the contrast between Christians and Jews be any greater? Thus the Jew 'according to the flesh' has become the epitome of rebellion against grace, and the son 'according to the Spirit,' the Christian, his triumphant counterpart.[26]

The result is sombre: the synagogue and those assembled there are represented as the shadow picture of the church, and 'Judaism' must serve as the negative foil to what is eventually called 'Christendom.'[27] With reference to I Thess. 2:15-16, it is actually affirmed that Paul was guilty of the anti-Semitism of his time, intensified by Christian elements.[28] Admittedly, this interpretation of I Thess. 2 can be modified to some degree when it is pointed out that some features peculiar to ancient anti-Semitism are missing from the apostle's words: the pagan reproaches of impiety, of ἀμιξία, and of disrespect for local and imperial laws. Instead of reformulating those accusations Paul speaks only of the opposition of the Jews (or merely of Jewish officials?; cf. I Cor. 2:8; Acts *passim*) to Jesus and the apostolic mission work among the Gentiles. At any rate, however, since the time of Marcion the latent or patent anti-Semitism which still pervades church and world claims to find support in Pauline utterances. The same man whom at first we attempted to introduce as a friend of the Jews and as a protagonist of the continuity of the one people of God, now seems to emerge as a traitor to and antagonist of Israel and a divider of God's people.

C. Attempts to Bridge the Gap

In view of the contradictory attitudes and utterances of the apostle, the question arises: Does the apparent tension in Paul has its roots in the psyche of the man, in a development of his teaching, or in the gospel of Jesus Christ itself?

1. By psychology

The affirmations of solidarity on the one side, and the radical demarcation lines on the other, have been explained in terms of psychology, as signs of an ambivalent passion: that is, of a love-hate relationship rooted in an indelible but thwarted attachment to Israel.[29] What the apostle has to say and to do in disapproval of Israel would then have to be understood according to Prov. 27:5-6: 'Open reproof is better than love concealed. The blows a friend gives are well meant, but the kisses of an enemy are perfidious'; or Ps. 141:5: 'I would rather be buffetted by the righteous and reproved by good men. My head shall not be anointed with the oil of wicked men, for that would make me a party to their crimes.' Paul may well be a good and righteous Jew—just *because* he condemns certain Jewish ways.

If this is so, then, the alternatives—that Paul is either philo-Semitic or anti-Semitic—do not apply to his soul, his work, his words, and least of all to his doctrine of the people of God. The abyss which at present divides middle eastern and western Christians because they read Paul with opposite results would be artificial if it could be demonstrated that nothing other than rapidly changing emotions were responsible for the apostle's contradictory or ambiguous statements. Certainly Paul no less than other people had the right to have and to express feelings of frustrated love.

But though such psychological explanations may seem appropriate to excuse or even to recommend Paul, they do not provide a means of dispensing with a search for coherence and consistency in his doctrine. After all, this man was charged and entrusted to give testimony to the righteousness and faithfulness of God and to the truth which is in Jesus (Rom. 1:17; 3:3-5; Eph. 4:21), not to his own better or worse feelings.

2. *By a process of development*
A solution by reference to a *development* in Paul's doctrine makes more sense. When this Pharisee was converted not far from Damascus to be a messenger of Jesus Christ, he did not receive and henceforth possess, as it were, a parachutist's full equipment which could simply be drawn forth and applied to all emergencies. Jesus Christ's revelation to him and in him (Gal. 1:12, 16; 2:2) did not have the character of fixed and inalterable dogmas; rather, just as is the case with other disciples of Jesus, so this apostle kept on learning while he was working and teaching. Assuming that both epistles to the Thessalonians and all the Captivity letters are authentic, the apostle's Christology and ecclesiology developed step-by-step from the Thessalonian to the chief letters (Romans, Corinthians, Galatians), and finally to Ephesians and Colossians.[30] Partly under the impact of Paul the whole of Christianity also underwent changes. According to a simplified version of highly complex events, the church developed between A.D. 30 and 90 from an originally Jewish revival movement to a community surprisingly extended by converted Gentiles and eventually to an assembly dominated by baptised Gentiles who were scarcely influenced any longer by Jewish elements.[31] Within the same decades Christology and eschatology, too, developed dramatically.

At any rate, in the Pauline epistles an evolution is definitely to be noted in the statements concerning the Jewish people and its relation to the church. Though the language used is picturesque rather than odious, the contents of Gal. 4:30 (which speaks of the 'throwing-out' of Abraham's son after the flesh) and of Rom. 11:17ff. (which deals with the 'cutting out' of the original olive branches),[32] still resemble the passionate indictments of the Jews found in Paul's first letter (i.e., in I Thess. 2:15-16). Yet, already in Rom. 11, Paul is concerned with restraining possible or actual boastful pride on the part of Gentile Christians: he reminds them that the temporarily cut-out branches may be grafted in again (Rom. 11:18-32). In I Cor. 2:8 and II Cor. 3:13-18 no more is said of Jews than that they are lacking knowledge and have their minds veiled. No mention is made of their being rejected; on the contrary, II Cor. 3:16 speaks of the removal of the veil. Paul had good reasons for never giving up preaching in synagogues. The peak of the development of Paul's teaching on the people of God is reached in Ephesians. Here the Jews' failure, guilt, and death in sin is paralleled by the Gentiles' misdeeds and spiritual death (Eph. 2:1-3; cf. 4:17-19). The baptised Gentiles belong in the people of God and are members of the church only because they, *together with the Jews*, have been raised in and with Christ from spiritual death. 'To be saved' means, for Gentiles, to be grafted into the people of Israel, to have part in the heritage which was pledged to the Fathers, and to rejoice in the fulfilment of the promise and hope which God gave to that people (Eph. 1:12-14; 2:1-6, 11-22; 3:6).

Because a certain development in Paul's insights cannot be denied, a careful reader and interpreter will refrain from fastening upon any particular dictum of the apostle and making it the one and only criterion for the interpretation and application of the apostle's writings. Rather he will follow the apostle and progress with him on the road which leads him to affirm that there is only one people of God, Israel, and that—by the grace shown through Israel's Messiah—Gentiles have become members even of this people.

3. *On theological grounds*
Besides psychological and developmental explanations there are more explicitly *theological* arguments to explain Paul's stance. First some Jewish, and then some Christian interpretations will be reviewed.

(a) *Jewish Interpretations*. Despite the traditional critique of Paul the apostate, though still with some reservations, a growing number of Jewish scholars attempt to see positive elements in the life and work of the apostle. In the (original, unrevised version of the) *Mishneh Torah*

('Law of the Kings') XI.4, Maimonides (1135-1204)[33] wrote: 'The teachings of the Nazarene and of the Ishmaelite [Mohammed] serve the divine purpose of preparing the way for the Messiah, who is sent to make the whole world perfect by worshipping God with one spirit; for they have spread the words of the Scriptures and the law of truth over the wide globe . . . ' Similar affirmations of the medieval poet Yehuda Ha-Levi, of the little-known nineteenth century scholar Salomon Formstecher, and of the famous Franz Rosenzweig might be quoted.[34] Leo Baeck has come a long way from radical opposition to positive evaluation of Paul.[35] To be sure, those Jews who appreciate the missionary function of Paul and of the church do not go so far as to assert that Israel and the church form one single people. However, the possibility is taken into account that the church, instead of being deemed a detrimental and cursed phenomenon, has its place in God's providence and is perhaps even a beneficial and blessed event or interlude in the history and mission of the chosen people.

Martin Buber developed the theory of a complementary relationship between Jews and Christians: each of the two, synagogue and church, is to uphold its own concepts of faith, which in the case of the synagogue is related to traditional, communal, and ethical matters, and in the case of the church more to individual persuasion and mystical unity. It was Buber's conviction that in the sacrament of dialogue, by mutual questioning and complementation, the two communities can co-exist in a way that is full of meaning and a blessing to both.[36]

According to H.J. Schoeps, Paul's position in regard to the Law is no reason for division and enmity between Judaism and Christianity.[37] He considers the apostle's statements on the Law as part of an inner-Jewish controversy which has its origins in the tension between Jews living in the diaspora and those living in Palestine. How could the Jew Paul proclaim the end of the Law (as he allegedly did in Rom. 10:4)? He considered Jesus to be the Messiah and the end of the old aeon as having occurred; the new aeon had no need of the old Law. Obviously, according to Schoeps, Paul erred when he asserted that with Christ *all* things had become new. But this error does not make the apostle a Jewish heretic. Rabbi Akiba, who considered Bar Kochba to be the promised Messiah, was not pronounced heretical, nor were the thousands of other Jews who were taken in by this or that one of the hundreds of messianic pretenders who brought dreadful tribulations upon the Jewish communities. Had Paul not introduced some Gentile

elements into his teachings on Christ and the sacraments, his work
and theology could be considered thoroughly Jewish.

S. Ben Chorin goes even further.[38] Just like every honest Jew, Paul
suffered under his failure to fulfil the Law; he *could* not believe in
salvation by the Law! Moreover, Paul's attempt to serve as a light to
the nations is evaluated by Ben Chorin as authentically Jewish.
Together with Schoeps, Ben Chorin tries to 'bring Paul home' into
Judaism. 'I love thee, the damned one of my brethren . . . O Paul:
prototype of the prodigal son.'

Again, Rabbi R. Rubenstein calls Paul his 'brother.'[39] Guided by
Freudian psychology, he tries to understand Paul as a person who,
during and after the process of adolescent maturation, had to break
with the authoritarian concepts of his time, and consequently also
with the Law of Moses, the Prophets, and the Rabbis. Rubenstein's
tortuous views, however, are mentioned here for their curiosity value
rather than for any theological plausibility and substance.

Brotherly feelings for, even sympathy with, Paul may be found
among contemporary Jewish readers of the apostle. Nevertheless, even
if Paul is recognized as a Jew, i.e. as a member of the Jewish people, the
critical solidarity just indicated has not yet led to the breaking down of
the wall of distrust, if not of enmity, between Judaism and the church
of Jews and Gentiles.

(b) *Christian interpretations*. Among the models created by *Christian*
scholars to represent the relationship between Christians and Jews,
again only a few will be sketched. All of them agree that there exists a
peculiar relationship between Israel and the church, and that this
relation is essential when the church is defined as the 'people of God,'
rather than as a sacramental, hierarchical, monarchical or democratic
institution. However, the relationship is described in ways that vary
greatly. At least four types are to be discerned:

(i) *Israel's replacement by the church*. Although in the Pauline writings such opposites never occur in discussions about the church, some
modern scholars work with the contrasts old/new, Pharisaical/true,
temporary/final when they compare Israel with the church. They
describe God's disposition towards Israel and the church more or less
in terms of a changing of the guard: once the Jews were God's people,
now the church is the true people of God. In this way the oneness
and uniqueness of God's people seems to be preserved—yet, at what
price?

Certainly it would be absurd to hear the tax-collector in Jesus' parable praying: 'I thank thee, God, that I am not like that Pharisee, now that I have taken his place in your presence.' It is no less ludicrous when the church asserts: Israel once was, but I am now the people of God; Israel's prerogatives have passed over to me, her sole heir;[40] although my foundation is in Israel, Israel has now found her fulfilment in me.[41] With such a self-understanding and in such words Christians have declared themselves heirs, successors or substitutes of God's (original) people. The latter then is left to its fate: it has 'crashed on the law.'[42] Nothing less than a monopoly on the blessing and heritage of Abraham is claimed whenever Christian scholars or church proclamations speak in such fashion. Then it is the church which has fallen prey to that self-glorification of which the apostle had accused both himself and the Jews.[43] By the insertion of chs. 9-11 into the epistle addressed to the mainly Gentile-Christian Roman congregation, and in his letter destined solely for the Gentile-Christians in Ephesus, Paul hoped to torpedo precisely such blatant triumphalism. 'Do not make yourself superior to the (cut-off) branches. If you do so, remember that it is not you who sustain the root: the root sustains you . . . ' (Rom. 11:18-24). The Apeldoorn working-group[44] which prepared *Nostra Aetate IV*, and the French Bishops' *Orientation*,[45] were quite right in explicitly rejecting the theory of 'substitution.'

(ii) *The Remnant of Israel.* Is the situation improved when some allowance is made in favour of the 'old' people of God in order to maintain at least a partial continuity between the old and the new people? It seems that a great concession is made to Israel when it is acknowledged that there is a 'remnant' of Israel (Rom. 9:27; 11:1-7), namely those Jews who believe in Jesus the Lord and Messiah. It is recognised that *some* Jews have been converted to him and therefore have citizenship in the (overwhelmingly Gentile-Christian) church. This remnant is believed not only to prove but to exhaust the fulfilment of God's promises to the descendants of Abraham insofar as children according to the flesh were meant. In order not to be suspected of Marcionite thought, probably all eastern and western churches are ready to admit, or even to confess, that even today through the Old Testament 'revelation' is transmitted to the church, that the church has received nourishment from the 'root of the good olive tree,' that the lineage of Jesus, Mary, and the apostles is Jewish, and that there is an enduring love of God for the Jewish people, 'for the sake of the patriarchs' as Rom. 11:28 puts it. Such formulations are found in *Nostra Aetate IV*, and I know of no contradiction or indictment of them by eastern church representatives. There is, then, an uncontested 'spiritual heritage' common to Jews and Christians alike. Surprisingly, however, and in curious proximity to the condemnation (in the form of 'regret') of anti-Semitism, the self-denotation of the church as 'the new people of God' remains even in *Nostra Aetate*. G. Eichholz and J. Moltmann[46] speak of an 'exchange' which took place between the former and latter ones, that is, between the noble and the wild olive branches. Though appropriate, the mention of an 'exchange' and of a 'remnant' does not really prevent the church from triumphalism and from claiming openly or secretly a monopoly on God's favour.

(iii) *The Schism in the One People of God.* A third solution is proposed by those who speak of a scandalous division within the one people of God which has resulted in the survival of nothing better than a 'split people.'[47] They are convinced that Jews and Christians have 'a different understanding of what constitutes God's people,' for each one of them 'lays claim to the heritage of this people's history since the days of Abraham.' This assertion leads to 'the question whether the claim of the one side . . . necessarily excludes the claim of the other.'[48] The French bishops speak of 'mutual comprehension' in the form of 'mutual challenge' and 'mutual recognition.'[49] J. Moltmann observes that Christianity and Judaism are each a thorn in the side of the other.[50] G. Eichholz, however, holds that Rom. 9-11 serves above all as instruction for the church from the example of Israel;[51] for the benefit of the church, Israel has to fulfil a unique and unilateral function: it poses a question to the church—while Christians apparently do not immediately have the right to answer with counter-questions.[52]

Is it, then, appropriate to speak of 'abiding values of Judaism' in the time after Christ? This formulation is found, e.g., in the *Orientations et Suggestions* of the Vatican Secretariat for Unity (chap. III). A warning about such thought and diction cannot be loud enough. For the talk of 'abiding values' shows little respect for and even less engagement with reference to Israel. As if the churches were in possession of a scale of values and were charged to make public the result of their measurements by pronouncing good or bad grades!

If, of course, the idea of a split people has any merit and is taken seriously at all, then its consequences must be that Jews will be invited to join the World Council of Churches and/or share in the labours of the Secretariat for Unity.[53] At the end of their *Orientation Pastorale*, the French bishops speak about the 'ever-crossing paths' of Jews and Christians. The relationship (to the Father and to each other) of the two prodigal sons in Luke 15, and the peculiar behaviour of each one of the unequal sons described by Jesus in Matt. 21:28-32, may well include hints regarding the factual and the expected relationship between Jews and Christians. Nevertheless, not even an ecumenical setting and co-ordination can heal the wounds of both Jews and Christians. Ecumenism notwithstanding, the abyss between Roman Catholics, eastern Christians, western Christians and Christians in the Third World has not been bridged—how much less is the chance to overcome the chasm between Jews and Christians! Whoever speaks of a 'split people' must be warned lest he confirms and cements the divisions as much as, for example, the 'Indian reservations' in the United States have done in ethnic, cultural, and economic regards.

(iv) *Complementary Existence.* The division within God's people is caused by guilt on each side, and the hope for a meeting and eventual reunion is far from being fulfilled. However, neither the split nor frustrated hopes need produce only a condition of distress. Why not make the best of a dreadful situation? When and where this intention prevails, the co-existence of church and synagogue in the time before the consummation of all things is not (only) considered a catastrophe or scandal, but (also) the result of a wise providence. Following suggestions made by Franz Rosenzweig, Leo Baeck, and Martin Buber a theory of 'two houses' was formed: Jews and Christians, the synagogue and the church, are in need of one another and can alternately enrich the other like neighbours in a lonely land. It is not even considered sufficient to speak of dialectic, dialogue, and mutual enrichment of the 'two types of faith.'[55] Among Christians, a justification of the continued existence of Judaism may be found in the fact that Jews sanctify the name of the one God, that they yearn for redemption of the suffering world, and that they attempt to take upon themselves—by obedience to God's law—the responsibility for the victory of divine righteousness here on earth, and do so at least as honestly and eagerly as Christians. In no other way can the task of the church be properly defined than in the way Jews glorify and worship God: the church is called and instructed to practise a worldwide mission in the name of God, to fulfil a ministry in view of the coming of God's kingdom, and to endeavour to do his will.[56] Both Jews and Christians are waiting for the Messiah—Jews for the Messiah yet to appear, Christians for Jesus the Messiah to re-appear. Such analogies in the existence of both Judaism and the church (which G. Eichholz among others observes) are unquestionable. From Israel the church may learn that only by grace is she in existence, and that only the hope for the consummation which is yet to come gives direction to her life.[57] For the time being the complementary model of the co-existence of Israel and the church appears to make the best sense. This co-existence is *pro*-existence: for the common Father, Creator, and King, and for one another and the world.

We conclude: The church's own life is at stake when she refuses to learn from Israel for what and from what man is living. Of course, the church needs no other mediator save Jesus Christ. But this Jesus Christ from whom she receives life, salvation, and knowledge is the sum and summit of Israel's history, and his body was and is Jewish. It is he who joins all Christians together with Israel. A fake or phantom Messiah remains the alternative to the son of the Jewish girl Mary, for only as the Messiah of Israel is Jesus Lord of the church and the world. For the church to declare herself independent of Israel and unconcerned about Jews would amount to rejecting Jesus Christ and preferring godlessness to salvation by the living God. The church cannot believe herself to be God's people unless she fully acknowledges her sisterly coexistence with Israel. Without Israel there is no people of God.[58]

Yet, according to the French Bishops, even the model of a complementary existence is contestable. 'Israel and the church are not two institutions which complement each other,' they write, though well aware that the present double existence of the people of God is a 'sign of the as yet unconsummated plan of God.'[59] The less than perfect is not a perfect solution.

Consequently, none of the proposed models for the description of the relationship between Jews and Christians is ultimately satisfying. Indeed there is no simple formula for the solution of all the problems existing between any human groups. Concepts such as substitution, remnant, dialogue, or co-existence (not to speak of continuity and discontinuity), are not capable of safeguarding a good relation between persons—be they men and women, parents and children, brothers and sisters, or fellow labourers in an enterprise. How much less, then, is it possible to comprehend and define by sociological concepts the people which is constituted solely by a third party: the Lord and King in heaven. Neither secular nor religious groupings, and least of all the interrelationships they form voluntarily or under duress, can supply perfect analogies to the mystery of God's people. This people lives from a secret; its history is not completed; the search is still necessary for what it is called to be and for the form it has to find. According to the Bible it is God's will, God's revelation, and God's call which make Israel, the church, and their connection unique.

Are Paul's statements on this topic, then, really self-contradictory or so obscure that different Christians can quote him in favour of opposite stances towards Jews? We shall attempt to answer this question in the next chapter in which we consider specifically the reasoning, the motives and the conclusions of the apostle Paul.

Chapter Two

THE TESTIMONY OF ROMANS 9-11
AND OTHER PAULINE TEXTS

The core of the Pauline arguments about the essence and identity of God's people is found in Rom. 9-11 and Eph. 2. Although Rom. 2-4, Gal. 3-5, II Cor. 3, and Phil. 3 also make important contributions to our topic, Protestant theologians tend to concentrate their attention on Rom. 9-11 when they discuss the Israel/church relationship. Although the whole of Eph. 2, and 2:11-22; 3:6 in particular, are devoted to this topic, the witness of Ephesians is pushed into the background, in part because this letter has been declared spurious and 'early catholic.' Roman Catholic research and documents, however, attribute to Ephesians at least the same importance as to Romans. In turn, the churches in the Middle East and in Russia react bitterly against both Western churches, for they discover in them too much eagerness to speak in favour of Jews and of the state of Israel. All western theology has been accused of being a 'geo-political theology.'[1] What does Paul actually teach?

We begin with four observations concerning the whole of Rom. 9-11; we continue with an outline of the structure and the highlights of these three chapters; and we conclude with a brief glance at some other Pauline texts. A detailed and complete interpretation cannot be presented here; in fact, not even all main questions and topics emerging in Rom. 9-11 and in the other texts mentioned can be discussed.[2] Instead, we search for an answer to one question only: What do these chapters say about the people of God?

A. Trajectories through Romans 9-11

1. The faithfulness of God
The whole passage Rom. 9-11 intends to glorify the faithfulness of God. The summation of the three chapters is indicated as early as Rom. 3:3: the unfaithfulness, *viz.* the unbelief, of 'some' (Israelites) does not cancel out the faithfulness of God toward this people. God's faithfulness is unilateral, free, sovereign, and it calls for faith and attestation. According to biblical reasoning, the free and irresistible

will of God does not exclude human decision; on the contrary, it destines and equips the chosen people for responsible action. God's election and call create and sustain, endure and judge, pardon and build a community which invokes and proclaims in one spirit the name of the one God.

Before Gentiles were granted participation in this worship, the 'Israelites' alone were made God's sons; only among them did the *shekinah* dwell; since the time of Abraham, it was with them that the covenants were made; to them the Law, worship, and the promises were entrusted; theirs are the patriarchs, and the descent of Christ is from them (Rom. 9:4-5). These declarations are not restricted to events of the past. God's word, once spoken, does not crumble under the impact of time, or of rebellion (3:2-3; 9:6); God has not rejected Israel (11:1-2); the whole of Israel will be saved (11:26a); the godlessness will be removed from Jacob, their sins will be forgiven (11:26b-27); the members of this people remain 'God's beloved' for the sake of the elected patriarchs, because God revokes neither his gracious gifts nor his calling (11:28-29).

What is the apostle's reason for impressing these points upon the Roman congregation whose members were mainly Gentile Christians? The answer must be: Only because God is faithful to Israel do the Gentile Christians have good reason to rely on him. Or, to say the same thing in negative terms: unless God proves faithful to the people he has chosen a long time ago, Gentile Christians now implanted into the same people have no reason to believe that their election by God is free from arbitrariness and capricious changes. A God who was unreliable in his relation to Israel could not be trusted to be faithful to any nation or person. Therefore, God's mercy over the whole of Israel is the basis and essence of the faith which confesses that there is nothing in the heights or depths which can separate those called by the divine love manifested in the Messiah (cf. Rom. 8:35-39).

2. The loyalty of the apostle

The references made in Rom. 9-11 to *God's* faithfulness find a surprising correspondence in expressions of the *apostle's* faithfulness to God and to Israel. Utterances of Paul about himself, and personal confessions introduce Rom. 9-11, interrupt them twice, and conclude them (see 9:1-5; 10:1-2; 11:1-3, 13-14, 33-36). Nearly all of these personal statements express a hope or have the form of a prayer. Paul is far from viewing God's actions as a mere spectator; nor does he indulge in abstract speculation. Were he to speak of God's faithfulness without giving any sign of his own faith, he would not be trustworthy. Only the faithful can speak convincingly of faithfulness.

Sincere and great emotion is apparent in the apostle's complaint about the hardening of his physical brethren and his wish to be able to save them, be it even at the price of his own life, which Paul like Moses (Ex. 32:32) would readily offer to God in exchange for theirs. The admiration he has for the zeal of the Jews is far from ironical; indeed, he himself has been a very zealous Jew (Gal. 1:13-14; Phil. 3:4-5). Paul is conscious of his descent from the Israelite tribe of Benjamin and grateful for it, because this fact has for him specific meaning:[3] it predisposes him for his missionary work among Gentiles.

The personal statements conclude with the adoration of the mysterious wisdom of God. Far from any arbitrariness, there is a liturgical order in the sequence of all of these pronouncements: they begin with lamentation, proceed to thanksgiving (related to the function entrusted to Paul), and conclude with adoration.

The faithfulness of God drives the apostle to recognise his responsibility and to work very hard. Even his activism, however, is characterised by his suffering for Israel and by his hope for the strength which God alone can provide. To recognise God's will is an existential act for Paul, including knowledge of the essence and value of his life. At the same time, knowledge of God also includes awareness of the origin, essence, and purpose of the church in Rome. Paul would not write about his relation to Israel unless he wanted all members of the congregation to share his insights and follow his way.

3. *Jesus Christ in the centre*

One single person (rather than an idea of his own, a general principle, or a blind fate) makes Paul an imitator of God's faithfulness: it is Jesus Christ alone. In Rom. 9-11 Paul quotes texts from the Pentateuch, the Prophets, and the Psalms which long before Jesus Christ's birth had announced a time when the dominion and the worship of God would be extended over the nations (Rom. 10:18-20; cf. 15:7-12). The advent, revelation, and work of the Messiah prompted the apostle to refer to those texts and to act accordingly. Because of his coming Paul knows that 'all men' are consigned to disobedience in order that God may pour out mercy upon all (cf. 11:28-32). Though in the concluding verses of Rom. 9-11 (that is, after 11:27), Jesus Christ is not explicitly mentioned, the substance of Rom. 1-8, as well as the first verse and many other sentences in Rom. 9-11, points to Christ as the centre of Paul's argument.

The occurrence of the formula 'in Christ' in Rom. 9:1 means more than support for an oath; it signals clearly that the following discourse cannot be understood except on the basis of its christological affirmations. To be 'outcast from Christ' would be, according to 9:3, the worst fate Paul can imagine. The advent of Israel's Messiah and the significance of this event is noted in various ways: 'his natural descent' is from the Israelites (9:5); he has come to reveal the sense, the unity, the purpose, and, above all, the fulfilment of the Law (10:4); he is the 'stone of stumbling' which was rejected in Zion (9:33); he is the life-giving word, the substance of faith and confession, the invoked Lord who is present wherever his people assemble (10:5-18); allusions to his crucifixion are made in 9:33 and 11:3; his resurrection is explicitly mentioned in 10:9; finally, he is the deliverer of Jacob who will come from Zion (11:26b). Perhaps Jesus Christ is called 'God' in 9:5; certainly in 10:9 he is designated by the divine title 'Lord.' All of these sentences proclaim Christ who is the same yesterday, today, and forever (Heb. 13:8); the one who is, was, and is to come (Rev. 1:8, 17-18; 22:13). His past, present, and future cannot be separated from one another when his work is described.

We observe further that in Rom. 9-11 each one of the christological statements depict Jesus Christ in a special relation not only to the church but also to Israel. The functions which are here attributed to Jesus Christ, especially the emphasis set on his original, present and future relation to Israel (Jacob, or Zion), deserve special attention. They forbid the notion that the 'problem of Israel' is discussed by Paul incidentally and for no purpose other than to exemplify 'man's' justification by grace, or to illustrate God's judgment over the 'pious' man in general.[4] In Rom. 9-11, God's chosen people—including the historical Israel which takes offence at the Messiah Jesus—serves not only as a *model* but also as an *instrument* of God's mercy upon all mankind. While in I Thess. 2:14-16 the Jews were depicted as murderers of Jesus Christ, in Rom. 9-11 they are denoted as the womb of the Saviour of the World and as the last recipients of redemption (9:5; 11:26f.). In the time between Jesus' birth and the parousia, it is precisely the hardening of Jews which brings about the preaching of the gospel to Gentiles (10:19; 11:7-22, 25, 28-32). Jesus Christ who has become the Saviour of the nations cannot be separated from the Jews.

4. *The use of the Old Testament*

In Rom. 9-11 the Old Testament is frequently quoted, and once, perhaps, an apocryphal dictum. As long as such quotations are viewed merely as a scholarly, poetic, or fanciful collection of 'proof-texts' or 'parallel-texts', their substance and function are misjudged. In fact, the allusions to Israel's history and to the promises, threats, and commissions given to this people serve a much higher purpose. They are intended to show that the history of Jesus Christ and of the nations is embedded in the history of Israel, continues that history, and leads to its fulfilment. Large groups of Protestant and Catholic scholars label this history 'saving history' (*Heilsgeschichte*). However, since this concept is linked to the notion of a 'new' people of God which takes the place of the 'old'—an idea which is completely foreign to Rom. 9-11—we will not mention it again.

In these chapters, the Old Testament quotations are meant to demonstrate that election by pure and free grace is neither novel nor provisional in God's will and action. They show that God's purpose stands fast although it is counteracted by rebellion and unbelief. They indicate that, even by the reduction of the chosen people to a mere remnant, unexpected multitudes are led to adoration. Finally, they reveal that both the Law and the promises given by God to Israel are perfectly fulfilled in Jesus Christ so that under no circumstances can the nations be saved without Israel or at her expense.[5] The indestructible co-inherence of the salvation of the Jews with the salvation of the newcomers from the Gentile nations is most strikingly formulated in Rom. 11:25-26: 'A hardening has come upon part of Israel until the full number of the Gentiles come in [to Zion], and so the whole of Israel will be saved.' The weight and the phrasing of this statement are so exceptional that it can be considered a pre-Pauline dictum cited by the apostle from a source he considered authoritative.[6]

After this perusal of four elements common to the whole literary unit Rom. 9-11, we turn now to the structure and some special traits of the individual parts of chapters 9-11.

B. *The Structure of Romans 9-11*

Leaving aside the introduction and conclusion (Rom. 9:1-5 and 11:33-36), the structure of Rom. 9-11 is usually presented as follows:

Part 1 (9:6-29): The Freedom, the Right, and the Power of God who Elects

Part 2 (9:30-10:21): Israel's Guilt and Fall
Part 3 (11:1-32): The Mystery of God's Actions[7]

In view of our quest for the essence and destiny of the people of God, we propose, however, different titles for the three main sections:

1. God's free election and sovereign faithfulness pertain to a people in revolt and keep it together.

2. The Jew Jesus Christ performs and consummates the worship which Israel failed to offer.

3. The good Lord made the unbelief of some serve the salvation of many.

These three parts and their subsections bristle with quite astonishing details:

1. *A people in contradiction*

In Rom. 9:6-29 Paul refers to events dating back successively to the time of the patriarchs, the exodus, and the kings. He combines a great number of quotations taken from the books of Genesis, Exodus, and the Prophets (esp. Hosea, Jeremiah, Isaiah, and Malachi) and sometimes comments upon them at length. His purpose is to show that God is faithful to himself and to Israel (9:6), righteous (9:14), glorious, and merciful (9:16, 18, 23ff.; 11:31f.)—when he constitutes, by his free choice and without being influenced by the 'works' of his elect, one single people formed of Jews and Gentiles (9:11-12, 24). In the process of Paul's argument the following steps can be distinguished:

(a) *9:6-13.* Since the time of the patriarchs, two kinds of children form Abraham's posterity. 'Not all from Israel are Israel.' It is God's prerogative to decide to whom his gracious promise applies. There are those who are no more than physical children of Abraham; Paul thinks of Ishmael and his offspring. But there are others: Isaac and his posterity owe their birth to God's promise and are called 'children of God' and are 'counted' as seed of Abraham.[8] Similarly Esau was hated by God while Jacob was loved. 'God's word does not fall down'— which means that even within the chosen Abrahamic community, God alone decides on election and rejection. Since among the people represented and begotten by Abraham, some are physical while others are spiritual members, some beloved and others hated, the conclusion is unavoidable: Israel, the people of God here described, is a divided people, a nation in revolt and in contradiction. What, for example, in

John 7:43; 9:16; 10:19 is called 'a schism among the people . . . among
the Jews' (provoked by the coming of Jesus, the Messiah), is described
by Paul as an archaic and intrinsic trait of God's people.[9]

(b) *9:14-18*. To the *internal* crisis of God's people there corresponds
a conflict stemming from *outside*: Pharaoh threatens it. However, even
this enemy becomes an instrument in God's hand; by his unsuccessful
rebellion against God, the Pharaoh serves as a witness to God's
overwhelming power and gives occasion for the worldwide proclamation
of God's glorious might and name. The ruler of Egypt proves in his
own way what Ishmael and Esau had already demonstrated: God is
merciful here and harsh there according to his own free will. But he
uses even the disobedient and rebellious for his purpose. When Paul
asserts that it is God who 'hardens whom he will,' he affirms—
together with, for example, Is. 6:9-10 (cf. Rom. 11:8-9)—that in his
freedom God assumes responsibility even for him who has been
hardened and proves stiff-necked, i.e. for the disobedience of his
enemies. It is he who 'consigns men to disobedience' (Rom. 11:32). By
bearing with the hardened, and by overcoming and using them for his
own purpose, God reveals the superiority of his mercy over all
rebellion. According to Is. 6:9-10 and Rom. 11:25, a part of Israel, too,
is subjected to this hardening.[10] To those chosen by God there belong
people whom we would call reprobate. God's elect people is not
unanimously and uniformly a believing and obeying nation; rather it is
threatened by external and endangered by internal rebellions. It is
precisely this menaced people that is carried in God's arms.

(c) *9:19-24*. Is God so arbitrary in his decision to harden some
persons and to bear others in mercy that those who are rebellious are
exculpated? Paul answers by reference to the authority or freedom of
the divine potter to mould different sorts of vessels. There are
masterpieces which are gladly exposed to admiring eyes, and there are
throw-away pots for base and menial use. Of the first products he is
proud, but the others have no future except destruction in anger lest
they ruin the potter's name. Have the latter a reason to complain?
Certainly not, because God himself 'has been bearing them in great
patience' for the sake of those which express his ultimate intention.
This potter demonstrates the results of both activities: that which in
his anger he *can* perform, and that which as a good potter he *will*
produce. Ishmael *and* Isaac, Esau *and* Jacob, Pharaoh *and* Israel have
been examples of such products. The assembly of people called from
Jews and from Gentiles in the church (9:24) reveals that God's mercy

over both, Jews and Gentiles, has been triumphant over his wrath
against the rebellion found here and there. The distinction and
separation of those elect and those reprobate, of the beloved and the
hated, proves now to have been a means to an end, not the final
purpose of God (cf. 11:28-32).

(d) *9:25-29*. With a daring last step Paul concludes the first section
of Rom. 9-11. Instead of further distinguishing between two groups,
those loved and those hated, the vessels prepared for glory and the pots
made for destruction, the apostle speaks of the transformation by
God's mercy of the reprobate group into the elect one. He does this by
the combination of two verses from the book of Hosea. By God's call
'Not-my-people' will be made 'My-people,' and this will be their name:
'Not-beloved' will be called 'Loved-one.' Hosea had preached to the
inhabitants of Israel (= the Northern Kingdom); to them he announced
their re-union with Judah (= the Southern Kingdom). For the apostle
the Northern Kingdom represents the Gentiles who will be united
with the Jewish people, like Hosea's Israel with Judah. An analogous
exegesis and application is found in Eph. 2:17. A saying of (the second
or third) Isaiah (57:19), originally addressed to *both* Jews living in the
land *and* Jews living in exile, is used as pertaining to *Jews and
Gentiles*.[11]

The quotations from (the first) Isaiah which in Rom. 9 follow upon
the Hosea texts form the transition to the next two sections. Israel's
reduction is again called to mind—as if to warn Jewish readers of the
boastful assertion: that to our own worth is due the incorporation of
Gentiles into God's people. The door opened to the Gentiles indicates
a judgment upon Israel rather than the strength or victory of Israel.
Only a 'remnant' and 'seed' of Israel is saved, and it is only because of
this remainder that Israel as a whole has not been destroyed like
Sodom and Gomorrah.

The statements made in Rom. 9:6-29 concerning the constitution,
essence, and unity of the people of God may be summed up as follows.
From its beginning God's people is in a continual crisis and schism.
But this does not defeat God; on the contrary, God's election of a
rebellious people, his love shown even for those not beloved, turns out
to be beneficial for the whole world. The part of Israel that was
hardened and rejected is the prototype, substitute, or representative of
the Gentile nations. At the risk or price of being thrown out of God's
house themselves, Ishmael and Esau, the rebels of the Northern
Kingdom (according to Rom. 9:30-11:32 also those Jews who take

offence at Jesus' crucifixion and at the gospel), keep open the door for the entry of the Pharaoh and the Gentiles into the people that praises God's name. Their very existence is like an urgent call going out into the world: 'A hearty welcome to you who are the hated and the hardened among mankind. Certainly you have failed to give glory to God. But look here, we are like you, and you are like us. Don't you see that it is only by God's mercy that anyone may belong in God's people? God who tolerates us, the reprobate and guilty, will also receive you into his people. Without you and without us, the riches of God's mercy would not be demonstrated and the seats at his festival table would not all be occupied.'

This summary of Rom. 9—a variation of the Parable of the Great Supper (Luke 14:15-24)—only *seems* to go beyond the wording and intention of Paul. It is, in fact, Paul's own conclusion in the text of Rom. 11:25-26. Thus, the hardening of a part of Israel is *instrumental* in bringing about the accession of Gentiles. The hardened Pharaoh (Rom. 9:17-18) has a partner inside Israel.

In Is. 40-55, during the time of the exile, similar things are preached. Precisely when and while Israel suffers God's judgment, this servant of God is destined to be God's missionary to the nations. It is not only the obedient remnant that serves God's honour but in its own way also the disobedient majority of Israel. The totality of God's people will be made up of that remnant, of the majority of Israel, *and* of the nations which will be joined to them. 'God has called us not only from the Jews but also from the Gentiles' (Rom. 9:24).

Some Christians have called the church a sacrament (μυστήριον), either because she is at the same time visible and invisible, or because she administers the sacraments and seems to be constituted by the complementarity of clerics and laymen. Not so the apostle, least of all in Rom. 9! This is the mystery of the people chosen by God: it consists of a variety of members all of whom are children of Abraham, the father of many nations. In his mighty love God embraces all of them, the obedient and the disobedient, the wise and the unwise, using each one of them as his witness. Even Not-my-people, or Not-Israel, is to become Israel, the Beloved. Therefore, the Old Testament people of God, as described in Rom. 9, exemplifies not merely a disturbing schism within the one people but also foreshadows final unity. Here, persons who are worthy of being condemned are confronted with a holy remnant and kept together by God, in order that all members of this people may become aware that they are chosen and united by sheer grace.

God's 'election by grace' may be described as 'double predestination,' since doubleness or duality is constitutive for it: not only Isaac but also Ishmael, not only Israel but also Pharaoh, not only some beloved ones but also all those 'not-beloved' are embraced by God's love. How could Paul depict God's people this way? His experience as a missionary of Christ among Jews cannot have created the conviction that even all those 'not beloved' in Israel would in the end be 'beloved.' Moreover, purely wishful thinking would form a poor basis for his theological reasoning and teaching.

In fact the apostle builds on other ground: in Rom. 8:29, where he first introduces the concept of predestination, he asserts that God 'predestined us to be conformed to the likeness of his Son.' What the apostle means by 'conformity to the likeness' of Jesus Christ is explained in more detail in Rom. 6:3-11; II Cor. 4:7-12; Phil. 2:5-11; 3:10, 21. In all these passages, conformity with Jesus Christ consists of participation and unity in Christ by sharing in his death and resurrection. Indeed, shortly after Rom. 8:29 (i.e. in Rom. 8:32, 34), explicit references are made to Christ's death and resurrection. In the crucifixion and resurrection of Jesus Christ, God's angry rejection *and* God's merciful acceptance are fully revealed: the horror of the former, and the amazing grace of the latter. This archetype of God's covenant with man contains in itself God's relation to his whole elect people. For Christ's death corresponds to the rejection of Ishmael, Esau, and Pharaoh; Christ himself was made an object of God's curse.[12] On the other hand, the 'acceptance' of the 'rejected' people is in Rom. 11:15 called 'life from the dead'; Jesus Christ's resurrection from the dead would be meaningless without the co-resurrection of a great people (cf. I Cor. 15:12-18).[13] According to I Cor. 2:7 (cf. 2:1 *var. lect.*) and especially to Colossians and Ephesians (Col. 1:27; Eph. 1:9-10; etc.; cf. Rom. 16:25), the mystery of God which is now revealed is Jesus Christ himself. In summary, the 'mystery' of the 'hardening of a part' of Israel and the salvation of 'the whole of Israel' of which Rom. 11:25-26 speaks is analogous, or rather, essentially equivalent, to the mystery of the crucified and resurrected Jesus Christ.

The following sections will show whether this Christological interpretation of 'double predestination' really corresponds to Paul's train of thought.

2. The true Jew: Jesus Christ

The main topic of the second section (Rom. 9:30-10:21) is not, as has often been assumed, an exposition of the failure and fall of Israel, although this topic appears at the beginning and the end of this passage (9:30-10:3 and 10:16-21). The centre of the text (10:4-18), however, is devoted to Jesus Christ himself and his significance for Israel and the whole world.[14]

The most important verse is 10:4: 'Christ is the fulfilment of the Law, bringing righteousness for *everyone* who has faith.' Here it is affirmed that Christ *fulfilled* the Law.[15] The translations, 'Christ is the purpose, the aim, or the sum of the Law' are equally appropriate; but the version, 'Christ is the *end* of the Law' (RSV, NEB, etc.), if understood in the sense of 'termination of the Law,' is misleading. What Rom. 10:4 affirms has its closest parallel and clearest interpretation in Rom. 3:21-22: 'Now, independently of (works of) the Law, God's righteousness has been revealed to which both the Law and the prophets bear witness: God's righteousness [effective] through the faith of (Jesus) Christ for all who have faith.' Probably Rom. 10:5 denotes *Jesus Christ* as the person who (according to Lev. 18:5) shall live, because he does what is written in the Law.[16]

At least four supporting statements surround the fundamental assertion made in Rom. 10:4-5: (a) Christ became a stumbling-stone to Israel; at this point Paul does not specify whether contempt for Jesus led to the crucifixion of Jesus, or whether the crucified man of Nazareth was the reason for the rejection of the gospel. At all events, Christ's cross and Israel's stumbling (and fall, cf. Rom. 11:12) are inseparably connected (Rom. 9:32-33).[17] (b) Jesus Christ is the 'word . . . near you' of which Deut. 30:14 speaks (Rom. 10:6-8). This word is the voice of the living God; nothing else grants and sustains 'life.'[18] (c) Jesus, the resurrected Lord, is the substance and object of that confession, faith, and prayer which assure salvation to all believers without distinction, i.e. to Jews and Greeks (Rom. 10:9-13). (d) Finally, it is the 'word of Christ' which is preached all over the earth by the apostles as the good news and as the invitation to have faith in him (Rom. 10:14-18).

Now, Israel took offence at this Christ, and Gentiles came to believe in him before many Jews did. But Israel's refusal does not negate the fact that the coming and the work of Jesus Christ accomplished for the whole world and manifested to it just what originally had been promised to Israel and required of this people: (a) the fulfilment of the Law, (b) the bearing of the curse by the trespasser (Gal. 3:13; II Cor. 5:21), and (c) the destiny to be a light to the Gentiles.[19] In short, Jesus Christ has fulfilled the worship and the mission to which Israel had been called. In him Israel's calling and destiny culminate and are brought to perfection. He is *the* Jew to whom God gives honour, and who leads Gentiles to praise God's name (cf. Rom. 2:17-29).

God did not, by the disobedience of a part of Israel, let himself be diverted from his faithfulness to Israel. Certainly, Christ himself and the preaching of the gospel, as well as the whole history of ancient Israel, is what is called (in Rom. 10:21) a 'stretching out of the hands of God to a disobedient and rebellious people.' According to the apostle and the prophets whom he quotes in 9:27 and 11:7, 25, the vast number of Israel constitutes a people lacking faith. Yet God does not let her be 'shattered':[20] rather he makes a native of Israel, Jesus Christ, the people's obedient representative, the one who before God and mankind meets the mark and fulfils the purpose of Israel's election. The stone on which they stumble is made even for them a foundation stone on which they can rely. They did *not* stumble over the Law, for Jesus Christ fulfilled it *for* them.

In Rom. 9:1-29, the people of God was described as a *corpus mixtum* whose history included both election and rejection until finally the rejection of the 'not-beloved' was overcome by the overwhelming love of God. In Rom. 9:30-10:21, Israel is characterized—in spite of all its vicissitudes—as a people which in its entirety exists no longer without the promised Messiah, but rather is perfectly represented by Jesus Christ.[21] His coming, history, and work prevent Paul (and his readers) from gazing exclusively at the status and behaviour of Jews as if Jews could speak for themselves and decide about their fate without respect to this representative appointed for them by God. 'People of God' is a functional and relational concept, rather than a static or self-supporting one. This people is manifest wherever, despite weakness and sin, there is a person who worships God truly, and wherever men and women from all over the world are assembled to bear witness to God.

It cannot be denied that the second section of Rom. 9-11 constitutes a 'shock-treatment' of Israel. But God himself rather than Paul (as an apostate Jew) is here at work as a healer. Paul might well have quoted (as does Heb. 12:5-6) the words of Prov. 3:11-12: 'The Lord chastises him whom he loves.' The negative argument of 9:30-10:3, asserting that Israel had not achieved by its own endeavour the righteousness in store for her, is followed in 10:4-18 by its positive counterpart: Jesus Christ alone has achieved what Israel was lacking. The section reaches a striking conclusion: while those first chosen still continue in their disbelief and rebellion (10:21), a 'not-people' or 'un-people,' even the Gentiles, have seen the light (10:19-20, quoting from Deut. 32:21 and Is. 65:1).

3. *The future gathering of the whole people*

The last part of Romans 9-11 consists of 11:1-32. Here it becomes obvious that the history of the people of God does not end with the schism in Israel, nor with the representation of the people by the Messiah Jesus, nor with the substitution of the former 'not-people' for the chosen Jewish people.

The section begins with a warning against a misapprehension. What was said in the polemical sentences at the beginning and end of the last section is protected against cheap generalisation by the apostle's return to the discussion of a 'remnant.' But whereas in 9:27-29 reference to a remnant was made in the context of the threat to reduce drastically Israel's numbers, now in 11:1-10 the positive function of the remnant becomes apparent. As at the time of Elijah so today, the remnant proves that only 'some,' 'a part,' 'those others' were hardened by God (11:7, 14, 17, 25). Considering the remnant which is 'left over' for God and to which the apostle among others reckons himself as belonging, it is preposterous to assume that God's people Israel is rejected as a whole (11:1-2). Far from indicating a renunciation on God's part, this remnant is in itself an appeal on God's part that is addressed to the totality of the people; it vouches for God's faithfulness to all of them for the sake of the Patriarchs (cf. 11:28). The acceptance and salvation of the 'whole of Israel' is and remains God's will and promise (11:25-29; cf. 11:12, 15, 23-24). God assumes responsibility, as was stated earlier, for the present drowsiness, blindness, and deafness of the majority of Israel and their consequences (11:8-10). How can they be overcome?

The answer is reached by a peculiar method. The central part of ch. 11 (vv. 11-24) confirms what has already, though more indirectly, been asserted in Rom. 9: unwittingly the rebellious part of Israel contributes to the accession and salvation of the Gentiles. 'By their downfall,' it is now said, 'salvation has come to the Gentiles' so that 'the world' becomes rich and reconciled to God (11:11, 12, 15). Instead of comparing God with a potter and Israel and the Gentiles with vessels, Paul now likens God to a gardener and the people of God, first, to a lump of dough (11:16a), and then, at length, to an olive tree and its branches (11:16b-25). The divine gardener acts in a way that a human horticulturalist would never imitate: he lops off noble branches in order to graft wild ones in their place so that these may profit from the sap of the noble root. The disobedient part of Israel has to give way to Gentiles in order to let them participate in the holiness of the chosen people. Up to this point the above-mentioned theory of succession or substitution seems to be validated. However, the beginning of this section (11:1-7) compels us to modify this theory by certain elements of the remnant-theory. Some of the original branches have not been cut away from the olive tree; it is only together with them that Gentiles may receive that holiness which makes of them members of God's people.

Nevertheless, the way which Paul describes is not yet completed. Two consequences of God's procedure are mentioned and discussed in a pastoral manner. The first is a development intended by God and a hoped-for result of the apostle's work among the Gentiles. The hardened, stumbling, cut-off part of Israel is to be made 'jealous' of the salvation which is now bypassing them and being given to the Gentiles. If only Israel could become 'jealous' of what she has lost and aim at regaining what she has forfeited (10:19; 11:11, 14)! The second consequence is absurd yet real, though it runs contrary to both God's and the apostle's intention. The Gentiles who were admitted to God's people are in danger of a cheap triumphalism at the expense of those Jews who at present do not (yet) believe in the Messiah Jesus. The boasting, pride, and (self-)complacency of the Gentile Christians is mentioned three times and reprimanded in sharp terms (11:18, 20, 25). Since everywhere in Romans (except in 2:17-29) and particularly in 11:13-24 the apostle is addressing himself to Gentile Christians, his pastoral warning against pride is stronger than his indication of Jewish jealousy.[22]

With regard to Jews Paul points to a future action of the divine gardener: God has the power and the intention to re-graft the cut-off noble branches into their original stem, even, if need be, at the expense of the foreign shoots (11:23-24). Thus the hoped-for turning to the Messiah by Jews, who up to now are lacking faith, will not remain a mere wish. After the crowds of Gentiles have come in, 'all Israel' will 'be saved' (11:26a). Because a remnant, the cut-off noble branches of Israel, and their re-grafting have been mentioned in the same context, the formula 'all Israel' cannot imply only 'the whole church' composed of Jews and Gentiles, but must include 'all Jews.' Whereas for some Old Testament prophets the (Gentile) nations' procession to Zion is the pinnacle of hope,[23] for Paul this procession is the penultimate event (for which he takes great pains to prepare, e.g. by organising the collection for Jerusalem).[24] His ultimate expectation is the advent of the 'Deliverer from Zion' who comes to forgive the sins of the children of 'Jacob,' i.e. of the alienated (Northern) part of Israel, viz. of the Jews who stumbled over their Messiah Jesus. Only the (re-)construction of the united, and therefore, whole Israel is for Paul (as in Ezek. 37 as well) identical with that eschatological resurrection of the dead for which Israel hopes (11:15). As if asked from where he draws this insight, the apostle answers in 11:25-27: it has come from a secret revelation (μυστήριον) which he has read in an apocalyptic book or which has been imparted to him directly and/or by his study of the Scriptures.

The doctrinal and pastoral statements of Rom. 11 are concluded in vv. 28-32 by the description of the dependence of the Gentiles' salvation upon the history of Israel, and of the solidarity between Jews and Gentiles. It is impossible that one should be played off against the other; for here as well as there disobedience has reigned, and for both sides there is no other salvation than by God's mercy. Solidarity, however, is not the same as uniformity. Solidarity has a long and eventful history through which God shows that, on the one hand, the Gentile nations are not saved at the expense of God's mercy upon Israel, and that, on the other hand, Israel is not saved without the extension of God's mercy among the nations. In spite of the disobedience and hardening of both Jews and Gentiles, God proves faithful to Jews and merciful to Gentiles. He carries out the intention of the original election of the Patriarchs, that they should be examples and witnesses of the rich blessings to be enjoyed by all families of the earth (Gen. 12:1-3).

The solidarity which Paul has in mind can be illustrated in terms of the relationship between the two sons in the parable of the Prodigal Son after the return of the younger (Lk. 15:25-32). This younger brother, first lost from home because of his malice and later admitted to his father's house by sheer grace, has nothing to boast about but much of which to be ashamed. Of course, the elder, by bragging of his works and endured hardships, reveals his own sin. But it is not up to the younger to tell him that, or to consider himself the only true son. Thus, Christians have no right to accuse Jews of self-righteousness and to regard themselves as heirs of the Jews. In both cases, only the goodness of the father overcomes all guilt, a father who loves both sons. On the other hand, neither the triumph of the father's grace nor its celebration can be fully enjoyed as long as the older brother remains outside in the dark and is missing from the festival table. It is God's will and promise that 'all Israel will be saved'!

The information gathered from Rom. 9-11 concerning the people of God can now be summed up:

(i) It is God's prerogative to decide who is God's people. This people is constituted by God's choice and promise alone; it is sustained by his faithfulness and power, judged by his righteousness, pardoned by his mercy, and made complete for his honour. Its characteristics and identity, therefore, are not determined by the inclusive or exclusive self-consciousness of either Jews or Christians, except perhaps by the recognition common to both—that each of them is utterly unworthy to belong in this people.

(ii) The existence of God's people in ever-changing Old Testamental, intertestamental, and post-Christian forms is indisputable. The election, judgment, preservation, and mission of Israel in the midst of the nations shape the history of the Jewish people from the beginning, in the present, and into the future. Therefore, the concept and the reality of God's people form neither a timeless idea nor a utopia or dream. Its peculiar, mysterious, incomparable, and purposeful existence defies any manipulation by itself or its enemies. Further, it calls for repentance within and outside its border. A particularity of the Jewish people consists in the fact that this nation has among its members representatives of God's enemies and that it will be saved and completed only together with the nations.

(iii) Furthermore, the history of the church, that is of God's people called from Jews and Gentiles, is unfinished. Just as in the past the identity of the chosen people was determined by the acts of God, so it will be in the future: the coming of the Lord, the resurrection of the dead, and the reunion of the dispersed members will determine its character, number, and life. By their eager waiting for the coming Lord and by their living hope for his gifts, and not by any boasting of a presumed possession, are all servants of God recognised.[25]

(iv) The unity of Jews and Christians in the church is a provisional and fragmentary representation of the one people of God, and in itself an urgent appeal to all nations and to the whole of Israel to gather in one house for the service of God.

This completes our discussion of Romans 9-11.

C. Galatians 4 and Ephesians 2

At this point an exegesis of Gal. 4:21-31, II Cor. 3, and Eph. 2:11-22 would be in order. These passages call for an intensive interpretation equal to that of Rom. 9-11 since they, too—though each with quite different accents—speak of the relation between Israel and the church. The description of Paul's special ministry in II Cor. 3 is not so immediately pertinent to the question "Who is God's people?" as to require the inclusion of an exegesis of this most complicated chapter in the present context. However, some summary remarks on the other two texts may at least demonstrate their relevance.

1. *The removal of Hagar and Ishmael*

In Gal. 4 (cf. II Cor. 3 and Heb. 8) Old Testament texts are quoted in the framework of a discourse on two covenants which differ widely from each other. According to Gal. 4:24-25, 29-31, one of these covenants (characterised by the Law) is personified by Hagar, the slave-woman of Abraham and mother of Ishmael, the other by Sarah, the free-born wife of Abraham and mother of Isaac. Typologically, Sarah and Isaac represent Christians (the free children of God's promise), Hagar and Ishmael Jews (kept slaves under the Law).[26] Paul reminds Christians that Hagar, her son, and what they represent, were 'thrown out' and disinherited, and that the firstborn son of Abraham persecuted the spiritual son, just as in Paul's days, the church is persecuted by Jews (Gal. 4:29-30). In this context Paul does not mention that according to the Genesis story God also looked and had mercy on the suffering Hagar, saved the life of the disinherited Ishmael, and promised to make a nation out of the son of the slave-woman (Gen. 16:10-15; 21:13-21). Rom. 9-11, however, proves that after the writing of Galatians Paul progressed in his thinking even on this matter.[27]

2. *The Naturalisation of the Gentiles by Jesus Christ*

In Eph. 2, the same theme is treated in a different way.[28] Regarding assertions about the people of God, some differences from the substance of Rom. 9-11 are obvious. In Romans, a split is assumed within Israel between the majority and the remnant, and between the hardened part of Israel and the church. Ephesians, however, speaks of a single people of God, of the citizenship of Israel, into which Gentiles have been accepted. According to Romans, the crucifixion of Christ apparently is the result and cause of the present schism among God's people; only in his parousia and by the resurrection of all the dead will Christ overcome the present division between the church and Israel. In Ephesians, the Crucified is acclaimed as the creator of peace and unity between Jews and Gentiles; no hardening of the Jews, no throw-away 'vessels of wrath,' no cut-off branches or thrown-out slaves are mentioned; there is no reference to Israel's foolishness, blindness, callousness, for all these forms of hardening are attributed only to the Gentiles (Eph. 2:11-13, 17, 19; 4:17-19). Instead of describing Jews as a people who reject the Messiah and the gospel, this letter refers to them as persons who, unlike the Gentiles, have hope (for the promised Messiah and an inheritance, Eph. 1:12; 3:6; cf. 2:12), who are circumcised members of a citizenship established by God's promise and covenant, and who are 'near,' 'saints,' and children in God's household (Eph. 2:12, 17, 19).

In Eph. 2, three things stand out:
(a) The naturalisation and adoption of Gentiles presupposes the destruction of the wall, built up by an interpretation of the law 'in statutory ordinances,' which separates the people of God from the nations (2:14-15). Just as in Rom. 9:12, 32 and 11:6, so in Eph. 2:9, a brief and sharp outburst occurs against 'works (of the Law)'; salvation can neither be sought nor secured by obedience to divisive statutes such as sabbath, circumcision, and dietary laws.
(b) The death of the Messiah on the cross is emphatically presented as the means of unification and reconciliation between Jews and Christians (his blood, flesh, body, cross are mentioned in Eph. 2:13-16). When, as in Rom. 10:9-20 and 11:13, references are made to the resurrection of Christ and the proclamation of the gospel, special emphasis lies always on the unifying power of these events (Eph. 1:19-2:16; 2:17;[29] 3:5-12). One of the effects of the (Holy) Spirit (who is not mentioned in Rom. 9-11) is to join together diverse members of God's house (Eph. 2:18, 22).
(c) The result of the peace made by Christ is the 'creation of one new

person' (Eph. 2:16), that is, the 'body' and/or the bride of Christ: the church.[30] She serves the Father in the Spirit, and her growth is described in terms of the building of a spiritual temple of God (Eph. 2:18, 20-22). This body, bride, or temple consists only of those Gentiles and Jews who believe in Christ and are sealed with the Spirit (1:12-14; 4:30). And yet, the sealing of part of the Jews and Gentiles reveals God's claim upon the whole 'circumcision' and 'uncircumcision' (2:11). It confirms and manifests the validity of Jesus Christ's rule, and of peace as well, for the whole creation (1:10; 2:17). Ecclesiastical existence is missionary existence.[31] The 'body' of Christ reveals his intimate concern for *all* bodily beings. The temple is not being built for its own or the building-stones' sake, but is planned and built for a great people. The beauty of the bride will shine abroad (5:27).

It has often been maintained that Ephesians (e.g. in 2:5-6) attests a triumphalist ecclesiology and an enthusiastic anticipation of the end-time. Accordingly, it is frequently repeated that the letter neglects futuristic eschatology and has nothing to say about the parousia of Christ. But clear indications to the contrary are found in the references to the (not yet inserted) keystone (or capstone) of God's temple (2:20-22), in the description of the development of the body as a growth not only from its head but also towards its head (4:15-16), and in the allusion to the yearning for the meeting with the 'perfect man,' that is, the princely bridegroom, Jesus Christ (4:13).[32] The epistle to the Ephesians knows about the imperfection of the embattled church; otherwise the admonitions given in Eph. 4:25-6:20 would be superfluous.

Essential elements of Rom. 9-11 are present in Ephesians, partly expressed in even stronger and clearer terms. But only in Ephesians (and Colossians) is the concept 'body of the Messiah' found.[33] Since the expectation of a Messiah promised since David's time is as Jewish as the physical body of the Messiah who has come, the church of Jews and Gentiles has no right to let herself be called 'body of the Messiah (or, of Christ),' nor to call herself 'people of God,' unless she recognises and acknowledges that she is participating in the history and community of the Jews. The Jews formed the people of God long before Gentiles joined in. He who would want to have peace on earth apart from the Jewish Messiah, and without community with the people of which Jesus is a native son, would separate himself from salvation. According to Eph. 2:1-10, there is no salvation without resurrection and enthronement together with Christ and with the Jews. An apprehension of salvation as 'individual redemption' is, for all practical purposes, excluded. In this epistle (2:1-22; 3:6) Christ's saving action is described as the reconciliation of alienated groups with each other and with God, not as the salvation of individuals. This does not contradict other Pauline letters which appear to lay the greatest emphasis on the faith of each individual. According to Gal. 2:11-21, for example, Paul's doctrine of justification was formulated for the first time in a situation where the unity, the common life, and, quite concretely, the actual eating together of Jews and Gentiles were at stake. And chs. 6-8 of Romans, with their very personal description of the life of those saved, are framed by Rom. 1-5 and 9-11, chapters in which we find described God's righteousness as revealed to Jews and Gentiles at large.

Obviously, our exposition of Rom. 9-11 is influenced by Ephesians more than by Gal. 4:21-31, not to speak of I Thess. 2:15-16. If Ephesians were missing in the New Testament, or if Paul had nothing to do with it (with the result that Ephesians would at best have to be deplored as a post-apostolic document), Gal. 4 might well bend the interpretation of Romans away from the testimony of Ephesians and toward the above-mentioned substitution or remnant theories. The eschatological orientation, which in Rom. 11 is decisive for all affirmations regarding the one people of God, might then be depreciated or ignored altogether.

The situation however is drastically changed when Ephesians is received and respected as authentically Pauline, or when Eph. 2, even if written by a disciple of Paul, is considered to be a competent explanation and continuation of Rom. 9-11, giving special emphasis to eschatological hopes which are in the process of realisation. In this case, not only do the theories of substitution or of a final split run contrary to Paul's doctrine, but also the restrictive hypotheses of a remnant and of complementation have to be radically modified. It is necessary and wise to regard the later epistle, Ephesians, as a key to the interpretation of the earlier, Romans. A man meets God only on the *way* on which God himself chooses to meet him, the way on which God leads and accompanies him. To accompany the apostle and to be led further on the way on which he was led, is certainly the best method by which to understand his witness.

Attempting to summarise the results of our exposition of Rom. 9-11 in other terminology we make the following assertion: it is not enough to say that salvation *came* from the Jews; for salvation *comes* from the

Jews (cf. John 4:22). Jesus Christ not only was a Jew—in the womb of Mary, on the roads of Galilee, Samaria, and Jerusalem, and on the cross—but he *remains* a Jew as the Resurrected, who intercedes for us at the right hand of God from where he sends us the Spirit and the spiritual gifts; he will be the same when he comes again.

These statements are not, as they seem to be, a diversion from the theme 'The People of God.' Too often the doctrine of the people of God—which should properly be called 'laology'—is overshadowed or replaced by ecclesiology. But at any rate neither of these doctrines is self-supporting. Christology is the foundation of both, and soteriology (the doctrine of salvation) determines all the traits by which the people of God is recognised. J. Moltmann has attempted to develop a 'Messianic ecclesiology';[34] we would rather call for the unfolding of a 'Messianic laology' which embraces *all* Jews, not merely the 'remnant' which believes in the Messiah already come. False decisions and attitudes, taken with reference to the unity of God's people, have the theological weight of Christological heresies; they are tantamount to a rejection of the salvation that has been granted. In Christians' relation to the Jewish Saviour their relationship with Jews is decided. In the relationship with Jews their relation to Jesus Christ is verified—or falsified.

Chapter Three

THE CHURCH AND THE JEWISH PEOPLE TODAY

What are the consequences of all that has been said so far? In listening
to the apostle Paul we certainly heard not only a message *about* Jews,
but also a call to seek and find a special attitude and behaviour toward
them. First we ask whether Christians are in a position so exalted and
safe that they possess the right and the duty to pass good or bad
judgments upon Jewish attitudes and actions. Then the question will
be posed as to which forms of gratitude correspond to the dependence
of the church on the election of Israel and on the continued existence of
the Jewish people. Finally, the challenge offered by the state of Israel to
both the church and all the nations receives special attention.

A. Separation by Value-Judgments

1. *Self-evaluation on the part of Jesus and the church*
'If I testify on my own behalf, that testimony does not hold good. There
is another who bears witness for me ... Not that I rely on human
testimony [such as John the Baptist's] but I remind you of it for your
own salvation ... I do not look to men for honour ... Whoever has the
will to do the will of God shall know whether my teaching comes from
him or is merely my own.' These words of Jesus recorded in the Gospel
of John[1] contain an unequivocal depreciation of assertions and claims
made in the form of self-evaluations.[2] How, then, are Jesus' authenticity
and authority recognised? Not by claims which he would make for
himself or which others would make for him; they are recognised in
ever new acts of faithfulness and obedience. Knowledge does not
precede action, neither is it related to activity as is theory to practice.
Relevant theological teaching draws its vitality from its reference to
God's own testimony, and learning about God and Christ is gained by
doing the will of the Lord. In Calvin's words: *omnis recta cognitio Dei
ab obedientia nascitur* (obedience is the mother of true knowledge of
God).[3]

What is good enough for Jesus is good enough for God's people and its members, unless the servant presumes he is superior to the one who sent him. Self-consciousness and selfish claims, a pretended monopoly and rose-coloured self-portrayals can never make any community the people of God, or any individual a member of God's people.[4] What G.E. von Lessing in *Nathan der Weise* meant to convey by the parable of the rings also applies to the right to bear the name 'people of God': only in the comportment and daily life of the three sons will it become evident which one is a true son of the father. According to Matt. 25:31-46 Jesus Christ himself, on the day of his parousia, will judge and make publicly known which are the sheep and the goats. In I Cor. 3:12-15; 4:3-5; II Cor. 3:1-3; 5:10; Rom. 2:5-16; 14:10, and elsewhere, Paul shows that he shares the same conviction. He knows that God's historical involvement with his people is as yet unfinished because the judgment day is still to come. All the time, from the day of the Damascus road, the apostle's thinking is 'eschatological,' and his preaching, teaching, and counselling are determined by fear of God and hope for mercy.

Accordingly, Paul's ecclesiology also excludes the claim that the church in, by, and of herself is the people of God. Being neo-citizens in the kingdom of God, Gentile Christians have no reason to deny that Jews belong within God's people. In Rom. 11 Paul gave a serious warning against such triumphalism. His lamentation about the Jews taking offence at Christ also differs from the kind of pity which would imply condescension towards, or even contempt for, an underdeveloped (senior) brother.[5] Finally, though Paul did speak of the firm and lasting promises and gifts made by God to the Jews, he abstained from making allusions, as though from a high pedestal, to a 'remaining relevance of Judaism,' and from statements conceding to Jews certain 'values' which would have survived the crucifixion of Jesus and the refusal of the gospel. He who, despite his own unfaithfulness, lives from God's faithfulness alone (cf. Rom. 3:3) is not dependent on value-judgments originating from the church. Whenever such assessments are made, they are due to a presumptuous conception of the church's ministry and need not impress anyone.[6]

What the church decries as signs of unfaithfulness and apostasy on the part of Jews she will find repeated and surpassed in her own ranks. In the church there are certainly at least as many 'vessels of wrath' as among Jews; in both communities they have not yet been crushed merely because God continues to bear with them, desiring to make beloved those that are still not-beloved. The harsh words which in I Corinthians, Galatians, Romans, and Philippians are directed against false teachers of the Law, as well as against libertinists within the congregation, show clearly that before God and fellow man no flesh—least of all Christian flesh—can be proud of itself.

Furthermore, Jews are not dependent on their existence being justified by the church and her theology. The miraculous preservation of the Jews throughout the millennia, the return of many of them to the land promised to the patriarchs, the rebirth of Jewish self-consciousness, and the foundation of the State of Israel show that Jews do not live upon the grace of the church. By protecting the Jews from extinction, despite their catastrophic internal divisions and the mass-murders organized by their external enemies, God speaks for himself and in favour of the Jews. Because God is faithful, we may speak of a *character indelebilis* of the Jews. Unlike other people and nations, they bear the privilege and the responsibility of being God's chosen people; this holds true whether or not Jews themselves, nations, or Christians acknowledge their special election. Not even the horrifying 1982 warfare in the Lebanon, and the massacre permitted by Israeli authorities, can destroy or limit Israel's election.

What is problematic, however, is the name, the claim, the existence of the church. Is this (in its majority Gentile Christian) body really the people of God? The certain answer is: only when it is incorporated in the people elected forever. It is the Christians' citizenship in that commonwealth that needs ever new justification and verification. In the time between the resurrection and the parousia of Christ, the evidence of 'the Spirit and power,' not of words displaying human wisdom, is the only valid criterion (cf. I Cor. 2:4). It is good that nearly all the above-mentioned documents (see n. 1 to Introduction) emerging from Western churches are free of missionary aggressiveness directed towards Jews; they address themselves in a pastoral way to the Christians only. It is pointed out with increasing vehemence that the Christians, while cherishing distorted, biased, prejudiced pictures of Judaism, have failed to ask for and acknowledge the self-understanding of Jews. Now self-critical Christians entreat their fellow-Christians to drop the clichés, to provide proof of better understanding and greater respect, and thereby to create among themselves and in their environments the presuppositions for a new relationship between the Jews, the church, and the nations, free of anti-Judaism and its hideous consequences.

2. *The Jews classed as heretics*
One of the prejudiced views which, as it appears, has as yet not been

renounced in any church document is the classification of the Jews among the heretics. In the course of church history reference has been made again and again to the description of the Pharisees and the Jews in the Gospels, to the persecutions of the early congregations, emanating from Jerusalem or from diaspora Jews, and to the polemics in the Pauline epistles against 'Judaisers.' In each case Judaism has been denounced as the epitome of heresy[7] more readily than pagan doctrines, cults, and patterns of conduct. Monarchian, Antiochene, and Arian christologies, with their misgivings and protests concerning the attribution of the title 'God' to Jesus Christ, were regarded as being equally heretical with the Sanhedrin's and the synagogue's rejection of the Messiahship of Jesus of Nazareth. In Alexandria, the historical and literal interpretation of the Scriptures was branded as a fleshly Jewish method. The synergism of Pelagius was judged and refuted by Augustine as a heresy which corresponded to the doctrines of the Jewish and Jewish-Christian antagonists of Paul. At the time of the Reformation the same Judaising opponents were rediscovered in the form of the Roman Catholic doctrines of salvation and the church. Classical Tübingen scholars and their modern successors have fostered an image of early Christianity in general and of emerging 'Early Catholicism' in particular in which the process of 're-Judaizing' is the principal menace to pure Pauline doctrine. Up to the present, a caricature of pharisaical piety and rabbinical theology dominates popular and scholarly textbooks used for the instruction and professional education of the churches' children, ministers and laymen.[8] 'The Jews' have been made the scapegoat for each and every misfortune inside or outside the church.[9]

What has happened cannot be undone, and there is no excuse for it. The church did falsely believe that she was serving the truth in Jesus Christ by educating the so-called 'new' and 'true' people of God to hate and despise, if not to seek to destroy, the 'perfidious' Jews. This hostile attitude towards Jews, however, did not save the church from the revival of old and the birth of new heresies and schisms, nor did it protect her from the indictment of complicity with Jews and from persecution by anti-Semites in the east and the west. In order to correct the injustice of anti-Jewish attitudes, the suggestion is now made by Christian, and even more strongly by Jewish speakers and writers, that a fair hearing should be given to disclosures of Jewish self-understanding, Jewish self-presentation, and Jewish self-evaluation.

3. *The Self-understanding of the Jews*

Where can Christians find, and how may they form for themselves, a just and valid image of Judaism? Judaism cannot be described either as a religion or confession and nothing more, or only as a culture or nation, and least of all as a race, although, in different periods, Jews as well as some of their friends and enemies have essayed to place Judaism on the same level as other historical phenomena. Interpretations of Judaism which abstain from the generalising concept of 'the Jew' or 'the Jews' appear to be most trustworthy. All too often generalisations are a subtle or crude means of manipulation. It is better to speak simply of 'this people.'[10] '*The* Jews' or '*the* Jew' do not exist except in anti-Jewish polemics or Zionist flattery; rather there are simply 'Jews' and the unique people formed by them. To speak of Judaism is to speak of the totality and the enigmatic community of all Jews which includes pious and secularised persons and groups, some living in forced or in voluntary physical or spiritual ghettos, and some pursuing cultural or political assimilation, including those who either set all their hope on Israel as a secular state or as a commonwealth to be determined by orthodox faith. Consequently 'Judaism' is an often self-contradictory entity which defies definition.

The Jewish people is marked by its long and as yet uncompleted history which has outlasted unspeakable catastrophes, a history of life *with* and *against* God, *among* and *against* the nations, and *for* their sake. Only in and by this history has the Jewish people a face and an address, and both of these are ever new and surprising. In spite of the claims raised here and there by a Jewish body to act as a magisterial or judiciary court entitled to pronounce generally valid definitions and decisions, there is nobody on earth who can speak for all Jews. There are, however, individual Jews, representative of this or that feature of Judaism; there are old and new scholarly books, resolutions, and institutions; there are Jewish traditions, Jewish liturgies, specifically Jewish prayers and signs of the faith that have been kept alive and have given strength to endure sufferings; and, finally, there are many forms of extremely passionate Jewish self-criticism. All of these phenomena of Judaism are authentic and deserve to be heard, understood, and respected, rather than to be perpetually ignored.[11]

4. *Contacts and Disappointments*

One method of becoming acquainted with Judaism is to seek and to maintain personal contacts with individual Jews, be they representatives of a group or isolated individuals, to read their books and articles, to arrange common conferences and publications, to establish academic lectureships and scholarships, and to provide chairs for Judaica in the framework of theological faculties and colleges. In these ways Jews receive at least a chance to speak for themselves and to be heard. Moreover, there is a need and a great number of opportunities for cooperation, at the congregational level, in biblical inquiry, in the sharing of historical information, and in social, charitable, and political action. Simpler and less costly ways of trying seriously to get to know Jewish self-understanding do not exist.

Even if meagre results or shocking failures again and again lead to disappointments on both sides, the corresponding efforts must not be abandoned. The shyness of some Jews to speak about matters of faith and the conditions laid down by those who will only or first of all discuss social questions or Zionism are not so forbidding as to prohibit open minds, hands, and doors on the part of Christians. The hope remains that by vital contacts the solidarity between Jews and Christians will be discovered, clarified, and strengthened, even if it means sharing in frustration and suffering because of inside failures or outside pressures.

This leads us to ask for guidelines and examples of Jewish/Christian co-existence.

B. Brotherly Solidarity

Paul's description of the history and nature of God's people (esp. in Rom. 9-11 and Eph. 2) compels us to speak of a solidarity between the church and Israel which takes up but goes far beyond the affirmations made in the church documents mentioned in n. 1 to the Introduction. These texts clearly witness to the covenant; to the one God; to the common root; to Mary, Jesus and the apostles, who were all Jews; and to the Old Testament, as bonds in the special relation between the church and Israel. It is good that the World Council of Churches, the Vatican Secretariat for Christian Unity, individual churches and church groups, and many a passionate speaker and writer enlist all Christians in the fight against every form of anti-Semitism and call them to abstain from cheap methods of mission among Jews. They plead emphatically for a relationship in which both partners listen and offer testimony to the other, in which questions are taken to heart so that mutual understanding and respect may grow.

The best formulation of these concerns stems from the French Bishops' *Orientation Pastorale* (IVa): 'The Jew deserves our attention and respect, often our admiration, sometimes of course our friendly criticism, but always our love.' Nevertheless, even this document falls short of the radical and full implication of Paul's doctrine concerning the oneness and unity of God's people.[12] For there is silence at the very point where the Pauline testimony is most impressive. The apostle speaks not only of a solidarity of the church with Israel on the ground of *past* events: he actually depicts the Jews as an *instrument* of God which is necessary for the salvation and consummation of the church. An instrument for the final end—this means that not only because of the past, but also for the present and the future the church is dependent on Israel and the Jews.[13] If there is reason to speak of *dependence*, then it is not only ungrateful and unkind, but also arrogant and false to call Christianity alone (that is, apart from Judaism) the people of God. The church originated by a schism within God's people Israel, a schism that will not be overcome by a victory either of Judaism over Christianity, or of Christianity over Judaism, but solely by God's victory over his split people. Until then, the church cannot do without Israel, and Israel cannot be without the church.[14] Because Jesus is a Jew, and because God has sustained the Jews up to this day and will sustain them until the end of the world, the Jewish people even today—and particularly for the church—is a 'covenant to all people' and a 'light for the nations' (cf. Is. 42:6; 49:6, 8).

We will now attempt to illustrate why and how the church, solely through continued dependence on Judaism, can truly be 'God's church' or 'Christ's church,' i.e., a worshipping assembly and representation of the people of God which fulfils its missionary assignment among the nations. While it is impossible to give an account of all dimensions of ecclesiology, we hope to exemplify the present significance of the oneness of God's people by considering four basic elements: truth, unity, mission, and worship.

(i) *Truth.* Judaism contests that Jesus is the Messiah. Convinced that with the advent of the Messiah the world will be transformed into a realm of peace, Jews do not see anything as essentially changed by Jesus' birth, death, and resurrection: the world is still unredeemed.[15] Do Jesus and the conviction that he is the Messiah therefore separate forever Christians from Jews? This could happen only if and when the negative attitude of Judaism was considered a justification for retaliation in kind. In actual fact, it is the very stance of Judaism which reminds the church that she has no other foundation and right to exist, and nothing else to confess, except Jesus Christ. Whether by words, deeds, or if need be by suffering, she bears witness to the 'truth which is in Jesus,' saying that now God's promise has been faithfully fulfilled and personified in the Jew Jesus (Eph. 4:21; John 1:17; 14:6)—or else she has no reason to exist. Though she has often failed to be aware of it, and though there are numerous ancient church books bearing the title 'Against the Jews' (see n. 7), all that the church is given to know, to believe, and to confess is at the same time 'revelation to the heathen and glory to the people of Israel,' as Luke 2:32 phrases it. When the church exults in Christ's cross and resurrection as the means by which peace was made between Jews and Gentiles then she lives up to her foundation and destiny. In her very existence and in her conduct, the creation of one new man out of the formerly divided Jews and Gentiles will be recognised. She is a temple with open doors for all mankind (Eph. 2:11-22). In this way, she supplies evidence of what she believes: that by the advent of Jesus Christ and his Holy Spirit, renewal in favour of all creation is taking place, already now. Consequently Jesus Christ can never separate the church from the Jews.

Sometimes the church fails to give true testimony. This is the case when for example she makes advertisements for herself as a psycho-therapeutic hospital for individuals, as moral power for the support of the powers that be, or as an institute for nothing more than social criticism. No doubt, the church has a function to fulfil in all of these directions, and she has done it for better or worse. But all of these things Judaism can accomplish just as well, or even better. It is, therefore, Judaism which urges the church never to lose sight of her foundation, her Lord, her goal—Jesus Christ—and to take ever new steps in her witness to the gospel, reconciliation, and peace for all. The church cannot look down her nose at Jews who are still waiting for the Messiah, because together with the Jews she forms a community of those who wait and hope. Who or what will prove that her faith and testimony are true? Certainly not monopolistic claims, but rather at present only the Spirit and in the future, with irrefutable power, only the parousia of Christ. Church and Synagogue are both 'Ladies in Waiting'!

If such humility and hope are essential in order to bear witness to the truth, the theology of the church is in dire need of some of the characteristics of Jewish theology. The latter is not based on dogmas nor does it reach its culmination in them; rather it is concerned with the Law given by God's grace and with acts of obedience which spring from an attitude of prayer. A Christian theology which abstains from thraldom to definitions and apologetics may find its way back to affirmations that are fundamental to it *and* to Judaism—such as *lex orandi lex credendi* or *credo ut intelligam.* Calvin's sentence about the relation between knowledge of God and obedience might well be recalled at this point. In following the lead of the Gospels and of the Haggadah, church theology might be well advised to learn again the form of 'narrative theology.' At the same time, according to the example set by the Halachah, though preferably without the casuistic tendencies of purely nomistic thinking, this theology might give up dancing around the golden calf of abstract concepts and rediscover that in all its aspects it ought to be so ethical and practical that no one could miss its personal and social, juridical and political import. A quietistic theology and non-directive ethics are ruled out whenever the Old Testament is properly respected as one of the sources and criteria of Christian theology, and when theologians are prepared continually to be advised and taught, warned and encouraged by the life, the suffering, and the hope of the Jewish people. The truth with which theology is concerned stems from and is contained in God's revelation which has made and still makes history; this truth is acknowledged and honoured only when it is being 'done.'[16] As long as the theology of the church considers the Old Testament and the life, the activity, and the suffering of Judaism as preliminary or even contrary to the search for God's truth, it will not be able to withstand the temptation of assimilation to, or the threat of victimization by, Greek, eastern, or western philosophies of religion.[17]

(ii) *Unity.* Up to the present, whenever serious steps have been taken to overcome the scandalous divisions of the church, contacts with Jews have certainly not been avoided or excluded; but the presence and participation of Jews in the actual dialogues on faith, doctrine, and order has been considered dispensable.[18] At best, this attitude is explained as follows: Truth goes before unity; whoever does not confess Jesus Christ as his 'Lord and Saviour' can neither promote nor achieve the unity of the people of God. However, it is being noted in Geneva as well as in Rome that at the present time progress in the efforts towards unity has come to a standstill. May that stop be only temporary! This present pause, however, provides an occasion to pay attention to the Pauline testimony on unity. The patient tolerance shown to the divided people, even to the hated vessels of dishonour (Rom. 9), the fulfilment of the ministry and mission of this people by

Jesus Christ (Rom. 10), and the future constitution and salvation of
the whole of Israel (Rom. 11) may yet prove to be signposts for some
further advances by almost stranded ecumenical movements. Because
it was hardened by God, that part of Israel which was not loved took
offence at Jesus Christ and closed its doors to the proclamation of the
gospel. But it could not escape God's wise plan and mercy, and it was
and still is upheld by his patience. Thus, according to Paul, even rene-
gade Jews contribute to the gathering in of the Gentiles and to the
formation of the complete people of God. Considering the promised
future unity of God's people, there is no reason to regard past and
present divisions as sacrosanct. The same is true also of the chasm
which still separates Jews from Christians, and it may mean that, for
example, the basic formula of the World Council of Churches should
be changed accordingly.[19]

To be specific: After the Vatican Council II, after the Meeting of the
Evangelicals at Lausanne,[20] and after the World Council's conference
at Nairobi,[21] a reconciliation of the Western Catholic and Protestant
churches can well be imagined in the (distant rather than near) future,
perhaps even a reconciliation of their right wing conservative-
evangelical and their left wing social-revolutionary members. The
basis for such a union might be found in the theology of Augustine, for
here biblical foundation, personal faith, sacramental and hierarchical
ecclesiology as well as political responsibility and application are
combined in an astonishing way. But Augustine's exegesis, dogmatics,
and ecclesiology were also influenced by some elements borrowed
from neo-Platonism and Stoicism. Who is going to preserve the
churches struggling for unity from coming to agreements based on the
pagan elements of Augustinian thinking, and from therefore constituting
nothing but a major Greek *symposion*? God has entrusted the Jews
with the commission to testify to the one God who has created heaven
and earth, and also to wait for the redemption of the whole creation
that still lies in the future and cannot be brought about by any
evolution, reformation, or revolution. Were the churches to despise
this testimony, they would never be able to find among themselves
true unity as God's people. Therefore the churches need Jews in their
deliberations on ecumenical unity, lest even Christians fall back into
paganism.[22] Contacts with Jews in which Christians prove to be
grateful recipients, rather than partners of allegedly higher rank, will
help to reduce or dispel at least two dark clouds: the suspicion of some
Jews that they may be regarded and manipulated as objects of mission

and conversion, and the fear of other Jews that a united Christianity may only bring new dangers and tribulations upon Jewry.

(iii) *Mission.* In western thought, predestination and the responsibility of free persons are contradictory concepts. In Jewish thought they are not: 'All is foreseen, and free-will is given, and the world is judged by goodness, and all is to the amount of work' (Pirke Aboth III.19).[23] The utterances of Paul are full of paradoxes if the interrelation and coherence of predestination by God and the responsibility of man is overlooked. The sovereign election and the unshakable vocation of God's people do not imply that this people is and has to remain passive. The same free grace by which this people has been selected from among the nations and saved out of Egypt and the Exile also moves and equips the liberated people to serve God. 'Let my son go, so that he may serve me' (Ex. 4:23). To put it in the words of Paul Tillich, framed in the course of a discussion, 'Freedom is only where there is destiny, destiny only where there is freedom.'

In the Old Testament, in Jewish missionary literature contemporary with the origins of the New Testament, and in some modern expressions of Jewish self-understanding (such as S. Ben Chorin's, see n. 38 to ch. I), the term 'service of God' has at least three connotations: it means to give honour to God by prayers; it implies conduct on the part of the members of God's people that is dominated by love of the brother and the strangers resident among them; and it signifies a priestly ministry for the sake of the nations. We have mentioned earlier the universal scope of the blessing given to Abraham (Gen. 12:1-3), the function of Israel as a royal priesthood among the heathen and as a light of the nations (Ex. 19:6; Is. 42:6; 49:6, 8). Briefly formulated: Israel's election determines and enables this people to be *the* missionary of God for the benefit of the whole world. Second Isaiah and Jonah in particular make it plain that it is not only when Israel is obedient to God that she fulfils this assignment, but also when she has disobeyed and suffers God's punishment.

When the church attempts to serve God in the appropriate way, according to the commission entrusted to her by Jesus Christ, she cannot help being a sister, a partner, perhaps even a spokesman of Israel. All she can do is to perpetuate the ministry of witnessing to God. According to Rom. 10 the Jew Jesus Christ himself, as the representative of all Jews, has fulfilled this service on the cross, on Easter Day, as preacher and as substance of the gospel, and he is still fulfilling it in order to bring it to perfection in his parousia.

This means that we have to bid farewell to a shortsighted interpretation of the 'Great Commission' (Matt. 28:16-20), of the missionary work and the success of Paul, and of the Acts of the Apostles. There was a time when the church understood her mission among Jews and Gentiles as a sort of propaganda and triumphalist procession throughout the world. A church that was feeling strong was tempted to follow the adage, *cogite entrare*, and to sing, 'Onward, Christian Soldiers.' There was and still is much talk of the superiority or universality of the Christian religion. Because at times the church equated herself with the kingdom of God or built edifices (allegedly) resembling the glory of heaven, she actually began to resemble an imperialistic enterprise, not too different from a multi-national business organisation.

The mission of Israel, however, was fulfilled primarily when Jews stood under duress, be it in the time of the Patriarchs, the Exodus, or of the later dispersions. Thus for Jews, mission means much more judgment and agony than triumph, whether secret or open. No one can escape the question, which missionary resembles better the slaughtered lamb of Is. 53 and the crucified Christ: the triumphal dame representing the church or the humiliated maiden representing the synagogue, as, for example, at the portal of Strasbourg cathedral? There is but one answer: both Paul and Peter served the Lord as *suffering* apostles. For a long time a majority in the church have tended to overlook this fact; but the illtreatment of many missionaries and young churches in our days forces Christians to return to the side of the suffering Jews. Only as brothers in a mission fulfilled under persecution and defamation can we prove faithful to the crucified Lord.[24] In her service to all mankind the church may confidently decrease, dispose of and renounce her glory. She may even lose her life for Christ's sake, since she is not an end in itself but a servant.

Similar things apply to the so-called 'mission to the Jews.' Probably a great majority of Jews resent the missionary methods employed by the church when Jews are actually approached in the manner of pagan people. There is *no* excuse for the medieval acts of force and ruse by which Jews were subjected to baptism. As soon as the church acknowledges her dependence upon the first chosen covenant-people, she will do penance for the injustice perpetrated against Jews during two millennia. An authentic testimony to Christ and a persuasive demonstration of repentance are given only when the Christian churches do much more than simply 'regret' or 'deplore' (*Nostra*

Aetate) what they have committed and permitted to happen. They are required to do all that lies in their power to see that discrimination, persecution, and murder of Jews is stopped and will never happen again. No longer can the church expect that Jews will be converted to and incorporated in a body that is still full of suspicion and hostility toward Jews.

Indeed, the church needs to work at her own conversion to the Lord and Saviour. Even a dialogue with Jews, whether deep or superficial, is in and of itself no satisfactory substitute for an improper 'mission to the Jews,' though the Constitution of the Dutch Hervormed Kerk for example speaks of it with the best of intentions. Nothing but the conversion of the church herself, analogous to the apostle Peter's conversion (see Luke 22:32; cf. Acts 10-11), can be the form and expression of the church's responsibility for Jews today.

(iv) *Worship.* According to the Gospels and I John 5:6-8, Jesus Christ submitted himself to baptism, that is, to a Jewish rite which was performed only among special ('sectarian') Jewish groups; and he insisted upon celebrating the same passover with his disciples as was observed by all pious Jews. We might say that what, at a later time, was distinguished as heterodox and orthodox conduct was still held together by him. He preached in synagogues, participated in temple festivals, prayed like a rabbi, partook in the singing of hymns of praise. Matthew's gospel contains logia of Jesus which affirm that he felt bound to 'fulfil all righteousness' (3:15; 5:17-19). Jesus' conflicts with the guardians of the Law do not prove that he intended to criticise or to declare invalid the will of God laid down in the Law; he questioned solely the 'precepts of men,' just as Paul does (see e.g. Matt. 15:1-20 and Col. 2:8). Paul's message resembles Matthew's when he speaks of Jesus Christ's 'obedience' (Rom. 5:19; Phil. 2:8), and when he declares explicitly that Christ in the days of his flesh 'fulfilled the righteous commandment of the Law' which no other man ever fulfilled (Rom. 8:3-4; cf. Rom. 10:4). Without such obedience, Jesus of Nazareth could have been neither the Messiah of Israel nor the saviour of the world.

According to the New Testament, a Christian congregation is to be found where people assemble in the name of Jesus Christ to invoke and proclaim the name of God in the confidence of the coming of his Kingdom, to hear the word of God from the Law, the Prophets, and the Writings, to celebrate baptism and the Lord's supper, to sing psalms and hymns, and where, both within and outside the community of the saints, they confess their faith by their words, their suffering, their mutual love and their socio-political conduct. Because the same God is adored, each aspect of the Christians' worship, whether in the cult or in daily life, has its precedent and parallel in Jewish worship. The worship offered in the church is based upon the confirmation, reformation, and fulfilment of Jewish worship by Jesus Christ and is, for this reason, nothing else but participation in Jewish worship.

This statement has a particular meaning for the administration and understanding of baptism and the Lord's Supper. It is not sufficient to speak of their origin in Judaism because their nature is still determined by their Jewish meaning. Every person who voluntarily gets baptised in order to 'justify God,' i.e. to give public proof of his repentance and hope (cf. Luke 7:29), and who celebrates the Lord's Supper 'as a memorial' and as 'proclamation' of the Messiah (cf. I Cor. 11:24-26) adopts and uses a Jewish form of 'serving' God. Only because it has been forgotten that without Jews we would not have our forms of 'sacramental' worship at all, have baptism and communion often been explained and celebrated as something akin to mystery rites or even to magic.[25] Jews invite and help us again to observe baptism as a personal act of repentance, hope and commitment, and the Lord's Supper as a joyous community celebration.

Similar critical statements could be made with regard to the usage of and respect for the Old Testament, the ministries, the social activities, and the political engagement of the church. Though today the people of God is divided, and though mutual suspicion, hate, and contempt are still characteristic of its synagogal, political, and churchly forms, nevertheless this people remains confronted with the same principal tasks, problems, and temptations. As the younger brothers, Christians cannot give directions to their seniors regarding the right relationship with the Father. But it becomes Christians continuously to let themselves be called to order by the Old Testament, by Jewish prayers and liturgies, by the very existence of Jews. There is no other way for them to be true to the one and only eternal Jewish High Priest, Jesus Christ. He, the Jew, has taught his disciples how to pray. Both the synagogues and the churches are 'houses of prayer' if they are used properly. It is not possible to pray against each other; but together we can pray, 'Our Father.'

We conclude this section by proposing a correction of the *Orientations et Suggestions* of the Secretariat for Christian Unity:[26] In view of the common worship of Jews and Christians, it is not only 'under given circumstances ... possible ... desirable' and commendable to meet

occasionally for 'a common encounter of God in prayer.' Rather is it
urgently required that at all times the common needs and gifts and
hopes of Jews and Christians be met by common prayer. It is not only
the first three petitions of the Lord's Prayer but this prayer as a whole
which contains the standard for the cult and ethos of the total people of
God.[27]

After this invitation to common prayer—to a prayer that will
include a cry for the gathering of those who are dispersed, for the
coming of the Lord, and for the completion of God's work—it seems
that only things of minor importance remain to exemplify consequences of the Pauline doctrine on the people of God. However, the
foundation of the State of Israel in 1948 has created a situation which
can by no means be considered irrelevant to theology, since in a new
way it puts the peculiarity of the people of God in focus.

C. The State of Israel and Christians

The four points just discussed might be ghosts or 'pies in the sky'—in
theological language, docetic—unless they are complemented by the
question of their *political* consequences. Among the principles of
interreligious dialogue formulated by Raymundo Panikkar, thesis
III:1 speaks of 'an assurance of the *purely religious* character of its
intentions and statements, so as to preclude the possibility of
connecting it with any other aim.'[28] This proposition, which certainly
prohibits the mention of political issues in discussions of faith, we
consider false, damaging, and impracticable. Christians who among
themselves and in meetings with Jews ask for the meaning and reality
of the concept 'people of God' certainly cannot evade the realm of
politics.

God has made his chosen people different from all other nations;
without that difference, how could Israel ever render service to the
others? Within the books of Judges, Samuel, and Kings as well as the
classical prophets, severe judgments are announced and recorded on
Israel's desire and attempts to be organised 'like all the nations.' The
policy of some rulers in Israel to trust alliances with foreign powers
and to suppress their own people by acts of despotism is called
defection and idol worship; it ends with the loss of Israel's political
independence.[29] However, before and after the Exile, some attempts
by the chosen people to endorse political elements from other nations
were regarded as legitimate and proved beneficial. Prophets, wise

men, teachers, and pious groups such as the Hasidim did not univocally condemn political accommodations but often felt free to support this or that development, so long as God's kingship was not negated.[30]

1. *Political Worship of Jews and Christians*

In the early Christian congregations, opposition to participation in political life was prominent only in times of acute persecution (Rev. 13). At other times, Christians were enjoined by sayings of Jesus and Paul to give the emperor what was the emperor's (Matt. 22:17f.; John 19:11), and to subject themselves loyally even to pagan rulers (Rom. 13:1-7; I Pet. 2:13-17). The stronger the church became, the more she began to take an active part in the creation and preservation of certain political systems and to share or even take over the responsibility for them. In doing so, she went through bad and good experiences in the same way as did ancient Israel and the Jewish people after the Exile.[31]

In Rom. 13 Paul speaks of the *Christians'* political ministry in terms similar to those used by his non-zealotic compatriots in prescriptions or recommendations addressed to Jews of their time. Has the apostle any special advice or directive for those among his brethren 'according to the flesh' who have not become Christians? In Rom. 9-11 and at other places he seems to have nothing to say concerning any future political shape or role of Israel. All the same, he speaks in Rom. 9:4 about the (still valid) covenants and promises of God, in Rom. 11:29 about the irrevocable gifts of grace made to Israel in the course of her history, and in Rom. 11:26 about the Deliverer from Zion coming for the benefit of Jacob. Paul was therefore more than aware of, for example, the promise of the occupation of the land, the tensions between the Southern and Northern Kingdoms and their resolution, the reconstitution of Israel after the Exile, and in particular the significance of Jerusalem ('Zion'); he was certainly very far from pronouncing any of these facts outdated and invalid.

What is expressed in Jewish prayers, before and after the destruction of the First and Second Temples (and down to the present) the apostle fully acknowledges: the faith and worship of the Jews who are promised and expect the Messiah is essentially related to the promised land, to Jerusalem, and to freedom from foreign yokes. He urges all readers of his letters, especially the Gentile-Christians, to recognise the abiding function of Jerusalem. Therefore, he arranges a collection of money for Jerusalem among the Christians dispersed throughout the world; he respects the congregation of Jerusalem as the mother church; and he quotes in Rom. 11:26 an Isaiah text (59:20-21) saying that the Deliverer will come from Zion. Thus, even after his conversion near Damascus, Paul acknowledges that salvation was first given to Jews in the promised land and has to be expected, again, from there. We repeat, 'salvation *comes* from the Jews.'

Now Paul certainly does not prescribe for present-day Christians the stance they must take toward the new State of Israel. Nevertheless, we may still ask for consequences and applications of his message, and we are in any case forced to take a position. The awareness that everybody has a part in the deeds and misdeeds of his religion, church and fatherland has not prevented but rather encouraged Christians of different creeds and nationalities to discuss political matters, however divisive they may be when Christians search for unity, and to begin to practise among themselves an ecumenical and spiritual solidarity. Jews and their state belong in that discussion. Christians cannot retain their prejudiced, aloof or neutral stance when the hopes of Jews for the State of Israel are at stake or else they and their churches will once again by their silence become co-responsible for, if not outright guilty of, the shedding of Jewish blood. How then, under the impact of Paul's teaching on the People of God, do we answer the question posed by Jews and Christians, Moslems and Gentiles alike: What do you think, what do you do about the State of Israel?

2. Changing Forms of Zionism

We start from the following facts: since the destruction of the second temple in A.D. 70, only a minority of the Jewish people has had the opportunity to live in the land of the Fathers. This minority, no less than the majority in dispersion all over the world, was threatened for nearly 2000 years—except during short intervals of relative security— with denunciations, persecutions, often even pogroms and massacres. Under such pressures, there originated, partly under the influence of messianic pretenders, during the Middle Ages and later, mainly among the Jews of Poland and Russia, 'Zionist' movements, aiming for the return of the anguished Jews to their old homeland. It was hoped that in the land of Israel Jews would be able to serve God in an unimpaired and perfect way.

Towards the end of the nineteenth century, new forms of Zionism arose. Zionism went through many secular and religious and often self-contradictory phases, and it had to overcome immense difficulties. But in 1948 it culminated in the foundation of the State of Israel on the territory of the formerly Turkish, then British-administered Palestine. The purpose of this state is not merely to safeguard the survival of the Jewish people after the murder of six million Jews in extermination camps, but also to secure the possibility of conserving and developing Jewish ways of life, be they religious or secular. Until the Six-Day War of June, 1967, this state was the hope of and the result of valiant efforts by a certain (growing!) number of Jews. Since then, and increasingly so after the Yom Kippur War of October, 1973, the State of Israel is a reality which affects, unites (and also terrifies) all Jews in all lands.

There are some reservations and protests on the part of certain orthodox Jewish groups such as, for example, the Jerusalem Mea-Shearim group; they do not recognise that the present state fulfils God's promises concerning Israel's final gathering because the Messiah has not come and the present return of Jews to their land is not yet, as it ought to be, marked by a total repentance and rebirth. Whereas in that schismatic group, as happened earlier among some groups in the diaspora, 'religion has developed into a substitute for the state,' and while the present State of Israel has become for many Jews an occasion to remember and rekindle the faith of the Fathers, for others it has become a 'substitute for religion.'[32] Between these fronts stand two groups: the Chief Rabbinate of Jerusalem, trying to use the government, against the protests of the secular majority of Israelis, as a means of establishing the Mosaic Law as the law of the land; and a political minority that attempts to alleviate the hardship and injustice borne by the Palestinians due to the founding of the Israeli state.

Among many members of the last-mentioned minority, the present situation is assessed in the light of the work of men such as the philosopher Martin Buber and the founder of the Hebrew University, Yehuda Leib Magnes. They hoped and laboured for a bi-national state. Indeed, Ben Gurion, on the occasion of the state's foundation, had spoken of the prophetic principles of righteousness which were to benefit equally all citizens of the new state, the 'Arabs' included. A considerable part of Jewry dispersed over the globe, especially American Jews, supports this promise and hope. On the other hand there are more or less radical groups fostering marxist-communist objectives. For a short period they have found support not only among disadvantaged, immigrant, 'poor' Eastern Jews and a number of Palestinians, but also from the 'new left' in the bourgeois democracies of the West.

But there are also strains other than the ideological ones: the sociological and cultural tensions between sabras and newcomers, Sephardi and Ashkenazi Jews, representatives of military and civilian ambitions and needs, and so on. The condition of war, interrupted since 1948 only by armistices and terminated only with Sadat's Egypt by the peace treaty made in March 1979; the permanent menace by near and distant enemies; and finally the inner tensions all explain easily why the present form of the people of God in the State of Israel is dogged by dangers, emergencies, and temptations, so that it resembles but little the fulfilment of an ideal. In contrast to the expectation of T. Herzl, the founder of modern Zionism, 'the state of Israel has not solved the Jewish problem as such, but at best has modified it . . . The Jewish state has become a partial aspect of the Jewish problem.'[33]

In view of the precarious existence of this state, it is impossible to consider the return of Jews to the land promised to the Fathers, the foundation of the Jewish state, or any of the present forms of Zionism as representing the realisation of the eschatological promises of the Bible. And yet, some of the hopes of Judaism have been fulfilled: a beginning has been made to make Jewish life more secure; astounding feats have been effected on the cultural, social, economic, military levels; no longer are Jews, at best, evoking compassion as slaughtered lambs, but they move on the stage of the world with their heads raised. Just as the worship of Christians and Jews is an imperfect attempt of humans to respond adequately to God, so is the Jewish state a far from flawless form of God's people. The increasing stubbornness of its successive governments, which so far has culminated in Menahem Begin's queer understanding of Palestinian autonomy, the annexation of the Golan Heights and the West Bank, the increasingly vicious supply of arms to some groups in Lebanon that call themselves Christian, the increasingly vicious invasions into that country can no longer be defended as a means to defend the security of the Jewish people. By thoughtful Israelis and non-fanatical Jews all over the world they are recognized as an all too quick assimilation of the young state to the worst sorts of nationalism, militarism, and suppression as they are practised, for example, in Chile, South Africa, and the two Koreas, by governments calling themselves Christian or Marxist.

3. *Critical Solidarity*
Because of the Jew named Jesus Christ, and because salvation comes from the Jews, a Christian concerned for Jews will affirm and support

this state. By God the Father, through Jesus Christ, and when only the slightest trace of the Holy Spirit moves them, Christians are called and enabled to say 'Yes' to it, and, despite all its problems, to defend it against its ideological and political enemies. This state is a touchstone for anyone who is convinced that God's people does and will exist in tangible form, rather than in the shape of programmes, ideas, or dreams only. As long as Christians—although they themselves and their fatherlands have been exposed and have succumbed to a thousand political temptations—do not give up the promise and hope of being counted among God's people, they have no right to deny Jews and their state the same promise and hope. Least of all has the head of the Vatican State the right to refuse recognition to Israel in the form of a state. With the measure by which Christians measure, they will be measured. Together with Jews they are under God's judgment.

The brotherhood and solidarity in which today's Christianity is united with the Jewish people rejoicing in the land and bearing its burdens cannot be exhausted in feelings and words of sympathy, but calls for attitudes and acts. Since, in the many forms of today's anti-Zionism, the old 'anti-Semitism' is continued or revived, the citizens of Israel and Jews dispersed throughout the world have the right to expect the Christians' support in their fight against every kind of anti-Semitism. In turn, this does not necessarily entitle Jews to brand any and all criticism of present-day political realities in Israel as anti-Semitism and thereby to dodge its hurting bite. Despite Jewish misgivings, a Christian should be permitted to view critically the policies of the Israeli right wing parties and of the 'hawks,' the cruel and damaging practices of the occupation regime in the annexed and occupied territories, the secret and public plans to reduce the offspring, the education and the material opportunities of the Arab part of Israel's population (such as the proposals made in 1976 by I. Koenig, the District Commissioner of Galilee in 1976[34]), and finally the atrocities committed and tolerated in the Lebanon war of 1982. Honest solidarity demands an appeal for more than mere caution when the brother is seen to be involved in unwise and often criminal deeds by which he loses his footing. The conscious ignoring of any rights of the Palestinians, the refusal to give them political freedom or at least total equality before the law, the equation of *all* branches and activities of the PLO with terrorism intended or perpetrated, the sevenfold barbaric retaliations for hideous terrorist actions, the lack of readiness for multilateral negotiations or any compromises, the plain lies and total warfare tactics used ever increasingly—these are striking examples. Confidence on the part of the Palestinians in peaceful coexistence is the key to a future peace for Israel.[35] So far, the State of Israel has hardly done a thing to win this confidence. How can Jews rely on the book that contains God's promises of the land, when at the same time they disregard its wise political injunctions[36]? The lack of a constitution reveals and aggravates the present situation.

There is, however, a minority in Israel that bravely fights for a total change in the attitude toward the Palestinian minority population. As in the early days of Christianity, so today, Christians of Jewish and Gentile origin, whether they live in Israel or elsewhere in the world, have occasion to show their concern and friendship for the whole of Israel by their special solidarity with the small group of Jews who stand up for the rights of those who are weak. We recall once again the summons of the French bishops. They ask that Israel be shown ' . . . our respect, often our admiration, at times certainly our friendly criticism, always, however, our love.'

Conclusion

The sum of the matter can be presented in six points:

(i) Jesus Christ did not come in order to divide and to destroy, but to reconcile and to unite. He died and was resurrected primarily for Jews, but also for Gentiles, so that both might be gathered into one flock. If Jesus Christ were the destroyer of the Law, he would in his person be the death sentence for the people that knows itself bound to the Law of God; he would be the first and exemplary anti-Judaist. Because he is the purpose and fulfilment of the Law for all who have faith, he has confirmed the election of Israel from among the nations and for their salvation.

(ii) The people of God is greater than the church. The church, the synagogue, and the State of Israel, as well as all secularised Jews, belong in this people and carry its name, because, since the calling of Abraham, even those who were not loved are sustained by God's mercy and patience. On the last day, God's faithfulness will overcome all unfaithfulness. Only together with long and still despised sinners will a man be saved.

(iii) No community may call itself the people of God or pretend to have a monopoly on this title. However, Jews and Christians are called

to prove that they are members of God's people and children of the
same Father by performing the service entrusted to them. God's
gracious election can be demonstrated only by the invocation and
proclamation of his name, by brotherly conduct, and in missionary
responsibility for all not yet aware of it.

(iv) Even by taking offence at Jesus Christ and by rejecting the
gospel, the Jews render the church a service for which she owes it gratitude, love, and respect. Without the Jewish people there is no church.
Conversely, the church is a detour for the salvation of Israel. Where
men meant to do evil, God meant to do good.

(v) Mutual understanding and engagement in dialogue are not
enough to demonstrate and strengthen the bond by which God holds
Christians and Jews together. The church owes her salvation to the
obedient Jew, Jesus Christ, and she continues to receive from Judaism
directives and warnings concerning her worship, her conduct, and her
missionary responsibility. Together with Jews she prays to God and
bears witness to him before the world, until Jesus Christ in his
parousia will speak the last word.

(vi) By the foundation of the State of Israel Judaism has given itself a
form which is to be affirmed and supported by the church. Excesses
within modern Zionism, including regrettable decisions and omissions
by the Israeli governments, are criticised by a minority in Israel. This
minority is entitled to the support of those Christians who are ready to
demonstrate their solidarity with Israel's temptations, sufferings, and
hopes, in order that the whole of Israel may be saved. With the
complete physical extinction of all Jews from the face of the earth the
demonstration and proof of God's existence would collapse and the
church would lose its *raison d'être*: the church would fall. The future of
the church lies in the salvation of all Israel.

NOTES TO INTRODUCTION

1. Among the outstanding *church documents* mention should be made of the following:

(a) from the *World Council of Churches*: 'The Christian Approach to Jews,' in W.A. Visser t'Hooft (ed.), *The First Assembly of the World Council of Churches, 1948*, London: SCM Press, 1949, 160-166; 'Statement on the Hope of Israel,' in W.A. Visser t'Hooft (ed.), *The Evanston Report, 1954*, London: SCM Press, 1955, 327-328; 'The Church and the Jewish People' in *New Directions in Faith and Order* (Faith and Order Papers 50), Bristol, 1967, 69-80.

(b) from the *Dutch Hervormde Kerk*: Church Constitution 1951, ch. VIII; General Synod of the Dutch Hervormde Kerk, *Israel und die Kirche*, Zurich: EVZ, 1961; 'Israel, People, Land and State'—a summary is found in 'The Church and the Jewish People,' *WCC Newsletter*, Sept. 1970; full text in German translation in *Freiburger Rundbrief* 23 (1971), 19-27.

(c) from the *Roman Catholic Church*: Vatican Council II 1962-65, *Nostra Aetate*, ch. IV, in W.M. Abbott (ed.), *The Documents of Vatican II*, London: Chapman, 1966, 660-668; cf. Cardinal A. Bea, *The Church and the Jewish People*, London: Chapman, 1966 [a commentary on the second Vatican Council's declaration on the relation of the church to non-Christian religions]; French Bishops, 'Orientation Pastorale du comité épiscopal français pour la relation avec le Judaïsme'; English translation in *Christian Attitudes on Jews and Judaism* 29 (April 1973), 17-20; Vatican Secretariat for Christian Unity, 'Guidelines and suggestions for implementing the Conciliar Declaration *Nostra Aetate*,' *CAJJ* Jan. 1975; *Erklärung der deutschen Bischöfe* (28 April 1980), ed. Sekretariat der deutschen Bischofskonferenz, Fulda.

(d) from the *Evangelical Church in Germany*: 'Erklärung der Synode in Berlin Weissensee,' in *Kirchenkanzlei der EKD, Berlin-Weissensee 1950*, Hannover, 1950, 257-258; *Christen und Juden*, Gütersloh: Mohr, 1975; Reinische Synode (11 Jan. 1980), 'Zur Erneuerung des Verhältnisses von Christen und Juden,' *Evangelische Theologie* 40 (1980), 257-276.

2. Among *scholarly monographs*, the following are pertinent: K. Barth, *Church Dogmatics*, Edinburgh: T. & T. Clark, II/2 (German original 1942; Engl. tr. 1957), 195-233; III/3 (1950; 1961) 210-226; IV/1 (1953; 1956) 423-432, 669-671; IV/3:2 (1959; 1962), 876-878; R. Bultmann, 'Prophecy and Fulfillment,' in *Essays, Philosophical and Theological II*, London: SCM, 1955, 182-208; cf. 'The Significance of Jewish Old Testament Tradition for the Christian West,' *ibid.*, 262-272; 'Christ the End of the Law,' *ibid.*, 36-66; W.D. Davies, *The Gospel and the Land*, Berkeley: Univ. of California Press, 1974; G. Eichholz, *Theologie des Paulus*, Neukirchen: Neukirchener Verlag,

1972, 284-301; J. Jocz, *The Jewish People and Jesus Christ*, London: SPCK, 1958; E. Käsemann, 'Paul and Israel,' in *New Testament Questions of Today*, London: SCM Press, 1969, 183-184; and *Commentary on Romans* (Eng. trans.), London: SCM Press, 1980, 253-321; H.-J. Kraus, *Reich Gottes: Reich der Freiheit*, Neukirchen: Neukirchener Verlag, 1975, 369-373ff., etc.; H. Küng, *The Church*, London: Search Press, 1971, 107-150, 141ff.; and *On Being a Christian*, London: Souvenir Press, 1967; see 114, 322, 350 for a discussion of the quotations from speeches made by Pius XI and John XXIII; F.-W. Marquardt, *Die Entdeckung des Judentums für die christliche Theologie*, Munich: Kaiser, 1967; 'Die Juden im Römerbrief,' *Theol. Stud.* 107 (1971); also *Die Juden und ihr Land* (Siebenstern Taschenbuch 189), Hamburg, 1975; K.H. Miskotte, *Het Wezen der Joodse Religie*, Haarlem: U.M. Holland, 2nd ed. 1962, esp. 450-456; *When the Gods are Silent*, London: Collins, 1967; *Das Judentum als Frage an die Kirche*, Wuppertal: Brockhaus, 1970, esp. 7-16, 28-49; J.Moltmann, *The Church in the Power of the Spirit*, London: SCM, 1977, 136-150; C. Müller, *Gottes Gerechtigkeit und Gottes Volk* (FRLANT 86), Göttingen: Vandenhoeck & Rupprecht, 1964; J. Munck, *Paul and the Salvation of Mankind*, London: SCM Press, 1959; F. Mussner, *Traktat über die Juden*, Munich: Kösel, 1979; J.M. Oesterreicher (ed.), *Brothers in Hope* (The Bridge V), New York: Herder, 1970; *The Rediscovery of Judaism*, South Orange, N.J.: Seton Hall, 1971; J.W. Parkes, *Judaism and Christianity*, London: Gollancz, 1948; *The Foundation of Judaism and Christianity*, London: Vallentine, 1960; *Prelude to Dialogue; Jewish-Christian Relationship*, London: Vallentine, 1969; E. Peterson, *Die Kirche aus Juden und Heiden*, Salzburg: Pusted, 1933; reprinted in *Theologische Traktate*, Munich: Kösel, 1952, 239-292; P. Richardson, *Israel in the Apostolic Church* (SNTSMS 10), Cambridge: Univ. Press, 1969; M. Stöhr (ed.), *Jüdische Existenz und die Erneuerung der christlichen Theologie*, Munich: Kaiser, 1981; P. Stuhlmacher, *Die Gerechtigkeit Gottes bei Paulus*, Göttingen: Vandenhoeck & Rupprecht, 1965; T.F. Torrance, *Conflict and Agreement in the Church*, London: Lutterworth, 1959, 284-303.

NOTES TO CHAPTER ONE

1. P. Minear, *Images of the Church in the New Testament*, Philadelphia: Westminster, 1960, discusses titles or images of the church, among which he lists (66-104) twenty which emphasise the connection between the church and Israel. Cf. K.L. Schmidt, art. ἐκκλησία in G. Kittel (ed.), *TDNT* III, Grand Rapids: Eerdmans, 1965, 501-536, esp. 517-518.
2. In Rom. 10:21; 11:1-2; 15:10; I Cor. 10:7.
3. Gal. 1:13; I Cor. 1:2; 19:9; etc.
4. Compare Acts 19:32, 39, 40 with Acts 15:22; also with I Cor. 12 and 14.
5. K.L. Schmidt, ἐκκλησία (see n. 1), esp. 504-513.

6. Gal. 3:23-4:7; Eph. 2:6; cf. I Pet. 2:9; Rev. 1:6; 5:10; 20:6.

7. Micah 2:5; Deut. 23:2-3; Josh. *passim*; I Chron. 28:8; Neh. 13:1. For further references, see e.g. Köhler-Baumgartner, *Lexicon in Veteris Testamenti Libros*, Leiden: Brill, 1953, 829, and L. Rost, *Die Vorstufen von Kirche und Synagoge im AT*, Stuttgart: Kohlhammer, 1938. While the Septuagint uses ἐκκλησία only to translate Hebrew קָהָל and its derivates, it employs the almost synonymous term συναγωγή for rendering both קָהָל and עֵדָה. The Qumran community preferred to designate itself as עדה, rarely as קהל. The New Testament congregation is called συναγωγή only in James 2:2. W. Schrage, 'Ekklesia und Synagoge,' *ZTK* 60 (1963), 178-202, seeks to demonstrate that in the New Testament ἐκκλησία signifies a demarcation over against the synagogue which is bound by and to the Law; cf. n. 42. However, because he fails to discuss the term λαός, he tends to over-emphasise the discontinuity and antithesis between church and synagogue.

8. Cf. Hos. 10:2; Ezek. 16:1-14; etc.

9. Regarding the affirmations to the contrary, made by G. Klein, 'Römer 4 und die Idee der Heilsgeschichte,' *Ev. Theol.* 23 (1963), 426-447; 'Individual-geschichte und Weltgeschichte bei Paulus,' *Ev. Theol.* 24 (1964), 126-165; 'Heil und Geschichte nach Röm. 4,' *NTS* 13 (1966), 43-47: see U. Wilckens' reply in *Ev. Theol.* 24 (1964), 586-610, and G. Klein's rejoinder in the same volume, 676-683.

10. The Rechabites, e.g. according to Jer. 35; the Therapeutae, according to Philo, *De vita contemplativa*; and the Qumran community, see esp. CD I 4; II 11; 1 QH VI 8; 1 QM XIII 8; XVI 8-9. About a dozen other groups are enumerated by N.A. Dahl, *Das Volk Gottes*, Oslo: Norske Videnskaps-Akademi, 1941; repr. Darmstadt, 1963; cf. J. Thomas, *Le mouvement baptiste en Palestine et Syrie*, Gembloux: Duculot, 1935.

11. Examples of this trend are the title and substance of D. Goldschmidt and H.-J. Kraus (eds.), *Der ungekündigte Bund*, Stuttgart: Kreuzverlag, 1962; see also K.H. Miskotte, *When the Gods are Silent* (1967). There is an Old Testament tradition which uses for God's relationship to Israel the image of a marriage-covenant (e.g. Hos. 1-2; Jer. 3; 31:31-34; 32:38-41; Is. 54-55; Ezek. 26; 23) and speaks of Israel's adulterous behaviour by which this covenant is broken. However, there is no reference to a letter of divorce (see e.g. Is. 54:5-8). Only Jer. 3:8 is an exception; but in this verse only the legal divorce between God and the Northern Kingdom, Israel, is mentioned—without reference to a divorce between God and the Southern Kingdom, Judah. In the same chapter (Jer. 3:18-23) Israel's return to God, together with Judah's, is announced. The annulment of God's covenant 'with all the peoples' and of 'the brotherhood between Judah and Israel' of which Zechariah speaks (11:14) in an hour of despair (cf. Ps. 89:39) does (according to other voices) *not* imply that the covenant with the Fathers, with David, and/or with Levi is renounced; see Jer. 33:20-26; Is. 55:3; Ps. 89:2-4, 28-37. Statements in the New Testament about the New Covenant, as found in the Words of Institution of the Lord's Supper

and in II Cor. 3 and Heb. 8, take up these Old Testament threats and promises. It is most unlikely therefore, that in the New Testament the term 'New Covenant' has a sense contrary to its Old Testament meaning. See, for example, Calvin's interpretation of Jer. 31:31, *Corpus Reformatorum, Calvini Opera* XXXVIII, esp. 688.

12.   Titles chosen from the mushrooming Jewish literature on Jesus include: J. Klausner, *Jesus of Nazareth*, New York: Macmillan, 1925; J. Isaac, *Jesus and Israel*, New York: Holt, Rinehart & Winston, 1971; S. Sandmel, *We Jews and Jesus*, New York: O.U.P., 1965; D. Flusser, *Jesus*, New York: Herder & Herder, 1969); P.E. Lapide, *Oekumene aus Christen und Juden*, Neukirchen: Neukirchener Verlag, 1972; R. Aron, *The Jewish Jesus*, Maryknoll: Orbis Books, 1971; G. Vermes, *Jesus the Jew*, London/New York: Collins, 1973; S. Ben Chorin, *Bruder Jesus*, Munich: List, 1967; and 'The Image of Jesus in Modern Judaism,' *Journal of Ecumenical Studies* 11 (1974), 401-430; W.P. Eckert, 'Jesus und das heutige Judentum,' in F.J. Schierse (ed.), *Jesus von Nazareth*, Mainz: Grünewald, 1972, 52-72.

13.   Pseudo-Clement, *Homilies* II 16-17; XVII 13-19; Engl. tr. in E. Hennecke-W. Schneemelcher, *New Testament Apocrypha* II, London: Lutterworth, 1965, 94-127, esp. 121-123.

14.   R. Bultmann, 'Prophecy and Fulfillment,' in *Essays Philosophical and Theological II*; E. Käsemann, 'Paul and Israel,' in *New Testament Questions of Today*, London: SCM Press, 1969, 184, writes, 'The apostle's real adversary is the devout Jew.'

15.   A discussion of the alleged anti-Semitism of the Gospel of John is found in, for example, J.A.T. Robinson, *Twelve New Testament Essays* (SBT 34), London: SCM Press, 1962, 107-251; E. Grässer, *NTS* 11 (1964/65), 74-90; S. Pancaro, *NTS* 16 (1969/70), 114-29; 21 (1974/5), 396-405; P. von der Osten-Sacken, *Ev. Theol.* 36 (1976), 165-172; R. Leistner, *Antijudaismus im Johannes-evangelium?*, Bern: Lang, 1973; J. Bowman, *The Fourth Gospel and the Jews* (Pittsburgh Theol. Monogr. Ser. 8), Pittsburgh: Pickwick Press, 1975. Light is offered on the contradictory results by R. Fuller, 'The Jews in the Fourth Gospel,' *Dialog* 16 (1977), 31-37. The Acts of the Apostles speaks of the killing of Jesus by the Jews in 2:23; 3:13-15; 4:10; 5:30; 7:52; 10:39; 13:27-28. However, the statement that the Jews, or rather the leaders of the Jews, removed the one who was sent by God was made (according to Luke) in the presence of Jewish listeners, never before a pagan audience.

16.   Rom. 9:31-10:3; 10:19, 21; 11:7-12, 28-32.

17.   Rom. 3:3; 9:27; 11:5-7, 25.

18.   Rom. 11:7-10, 25; II Cor. 3:14; cf. Is. 6:9-10; Matt. 13:14; Acts 13:40-41; 28:26-27. However, in Mark 6:52 the disciples, and in Eph. 4:18 the Gentiles, are called 'hardened.'

19.   In Rom. 10:2-3, 19, the significance of 'not knowing' or 'ignorance' is presumably 'ignoring.' But cf. I Cor. 2:8; II Cor. 3:13 (also John 9:40; 12:40; Acts 13:27; and the less than securely attested verse, Luke 23:24, 'Father, forgive them, for they know not what they do').

20. Up to the present, the attitude of the Eastern churches appears to be determined by such words as John Chrysostom's eight *Homilies against the Jews* (Migne, *Patrologia Graeca* XLVIII, 843-942); to a large extent, they resemble a hate-song. This church father intended to discourage the members of his congregation in Antioch from visiting the synagogue, a thing they liked to do. A similarly important and representative Western document is Augustine's *Tractate against the Jews* (Migne, *Patrologia Latina* XVII, 51-64) in which—notwithstanding the fulminations against the Jews—some signs of love may yet be discovered. A survey on ancient church, medieval, and Renaissance utterances against the Jews is offered by A.L. Williams, *Adversus Judaeos*, Cambridge: Univ. Press, 1935. All phases of pertinent developments are discussed in K.-H. Rengstorf and S. von Kortzfleisch, *Kirche und Synagoge* I-II, Stuttgart: Ernst Klett Verlag, 1968, 1970, 288. Cf. n. 7 to Chapter III, below.

21. Cf. for example the objections to *Nostra Aetate* IV and the *Pastoral Orientation* of the French Bishops (1973), collected by J.M. Oesterreicher in *Freiburger Rundbrief* 25 (1973), 28-31, 33-36. Similar unpublished materials will be mentioned in n. 1 to Chapter 2. A joint statement of Eastern and Western theologians, asserting that the privileges of Israel were terminated, was issued at Zagorsk after the Six Day War, in 1967, by the Christian Peace Conference. The text was published in, for example, *Christian Peace Conference*, 25 August 1967, Prague, and *Junge Kirche* 28, Bremen 1967, 453-454.

22. In Rom. 2:17-24; 9:30-10:2; Phil. 3:4-9, Jews; in Rom. 3:21-31 (also in 14:1-15:6?); Gal. 2:3-5, 11-21; 5:1-12, Judaising Christians (of partly Jewish, partly pagan extraction) are accused of insisting upon 'righteousness by works of law' or upon 'self-righteousness.'

23. Paul designates by περιτομή not only the Jewish rite but also the Jewish people.

24. This is the way Rom. 9:28 is translated in the Zurich Bible, though not in the Jerusalem Bible, the New English Bible, and the German New Testament translation by U. Wilckens (1970).

25. Rom. 4; 9:6-29; Gal. 3:6-29; 4:1-11, 21-31.

26. I Cor. 10:18; Rom. 9:8; Gal. 4:29.

27. Cf. J. Moltmann, *The Church in the Power of the Spirit*, 136-140.

28. E. Käsemann, 'Paul and Israel' (see n. 1 to Chapter 1), 84-85. Essential features of this anti-Semitism are described by, among others, A. von Harnack, *Mission und Ausbreitung* I, Leipzig: Hinrichs, 4th ed. 1924, 259-289 (Engl. tr. of 1st ed. *The Mission and Expansion of Christianity*, London/New York: Williams & Norgate, 1908, 240-265, and in W. Bousset, *Religion des Judentums*, Tübingen: Mohr, 3rd ed., 1926, 75-76, 93. The proposition that Paul was an anti-Semite is refuted in W. Eckert, N. Levinson, and M. Stöhr (eds.), *Antijudaismus im Neuen Testament?*, Munich: Kaiser, 1967, 50ff., 82ff., and in M. Barth, 'Was Paul an anti-Semite?' in *Israel and the Church*, Richmond: John Knox Press, 1969, 43-78; 'St. Paul—A Good Jew,' *Horizons in Biblical Theology* 1, Pittsburgh, 1979, 7-45.

29.   Cf. D.E.H. Whiteley, *The Theology of St. Paul*, Oxford: Blackwell, 1964, 76.

30.   See, e.g., J. Coppens, 'L'état présent des études pauliniennes,' *ETL* 32, 1956, 363-372; L. Cerfaux, *The Church in the Theology of St. Paul*, London/Edinburgh: Herder & Herder, 1959.

31.   J. Moltmann, *The Church in the Power of the Spirit*, 141-144, discusses and criticises this thesis. On 141-142 he sums up E. Peterson's view in a form which goes far beyond Peterson's intention as expressed in his work mentioned in n. 1 to Chapter I. See also P. Richardson, *Israel in the Apostolic Church* (SNTSMS 10), Cambridge: University Press, 1969.

32.   Similarly wild thoughts have been uttered by pious Jews whose words were eventually given canonical status. See, for instance, Pss. 69:21-27; 109:1-19, 27-29.

33.   Following information graciously given by Rabbi I.M. Levinson in Basel, Maimonides' uncensored work is accessible in Oxford, under the sigla Neubauer 568, 591, and 610; it was edited by Irta Scheiber Sandor and published by Magyar Hellenikon (Press) in Budapest, 1980 (the quoted text on the second to last page); among the scholarly discussions of the Laws of the Kings, Kaharna K. (Kallmann), Jerusalem 1957, was mentioned. We quote the Maimonides text in the version offered by S.S. Schwarzschild, 'Judaism, Scripture and Ecumenism,' in L. Swidler (ed.), *Scripture and Ecumenism*, Pittsburgh: Duquesne Univ. Press, 1965, 111-132, esp. 131.

34.   Yehuda Ha-Levi (born in 1085 in Castilia) *Kusari* IV 23, ed. by I. Heinemann, Oxford: Phaidon Press, 1947, 121. S. Formstecher's book, *Die Religion des Geistes* was published in 1841; see esp. 365. Among the works of F. Rosenzweig, *The Star of Redemption*, London: Routledge and Kegan Paul, 1971, 351-353, cf. 413-417, is pertinent to the issue at hand. The affirmations of these authors are discussed by among others H.-J. Schoeps, *The Jewish-Christian Argument*, London: Faber & Faber, 1963, 13-15, 59, 63-69, 107-116, 128-145, and by K.H. Miskotte, *Das Judentum als Frage* (see n. 1 to Chapter 1), 34ff.

35.   It is worthwhile to compare the different judgments on Paul—first radical refutation, then careful, though critical approval—in L. Baeck's *Wesen des Christentums*, Frankfurt: Kauffmann, 1905, 1922, 78, 183, 295, etc., and in his essay, 'The Faith of Paul,' *Journal of Jewish Studies* 3 (1925), 93-110; see R. Mayer, *Christentum und Judentum in der Schau Leo Baecks*, Stuttgart: Kohlhammer, 1961, esp. 58-75. In his book, *From Jesus to Paul*, London: Macmillan, 1943 (reprinted Boston: Beacon Press, 1961), J. Klausner, too, epitomises the progress of Jewish research in Paul.

36.   M. Buber, *Two Types of Faith*, London: Routledge and Kegan Paul, 1951.

37.   H.-J. Schoeps, *Paul*, London: Lutterworth Press, 1961, 24-32, 66-70, 171-173. This book ends (293) with a reference to the 'rescue' of the heretic Paul. In the German original, the untranslatable term *Heimholung* says much

more than the English 'rescue'; perhaps the action of a father or older brother who makes a maligned boy come home is meant by it.
38. S. Ben Chorin, *Paulus*, Munich: List, 1970, esp. 16, 60ff., 77-78, 204-214.
39. R. Rubenstein, *My Brother Paul*, New York: Harper and Row, 1972.
40. H. Ridderbos, *Paul: An Outline of his Theology*, London: SPCK, 1977, 332. H.-J. Schoeps, *Paul*, 241, too, believes that the 'predicate of election applicable to the Israel κατὰ σάρκα has now been transferred to the new Ἰσραὴλ τοῦ Θεοῦ, the church.
41. Cf. P. Althaus, *Die letzten Dinge*, Gütersloh: Bertelsmann, 1933, 301ff.
42. R. Bultmann, 'Prophecy and Fulfillment' (see n. 1 to Chapter I), 182ff. W. Schrage, 'Ekklesia und Synagoge,' (see n. 7 to Chapter I), 196-202, asserts that the church called herself ἐκκλησία in order to distinguish herself from both the legalistic synagogue and the Hellenistic mystery-cult associations. In the choice of ἐκκλησία he sees an experssion neither of continuity with Israel nor of legitimate successorship to the Old Testament covenant people.
43. Rom. 2:17-29; cf. 9:30-10:3; Phil. 3:3-7.
44. See *Lexikon für Theologie und Kirche*, Zweites Vatikan. Konzil II (1967), 413.
45. In their *Orientation* IVb. K. Kupisch, 'Nach Auschwitz,' in H. Gollwitzer and E. Sterling (eds.), *Das gespaltene Gottesvolk*, Stuttgart: Kreuz-Verlag, 1966, 284-287, 285, affirms 'The church of Jesus Christ . . . has not replaced Israel'; J. Moltmann, *The Church in the Power of the Spirit*, 148, shares this insight.
46. G. Eichholz, *Theologie des Paulus*, 298-299; J. Moltmann, *The Church in the Power of the Spirit*, 141-144.
47. K.H. Miskotte, *Das Judentum als Frage*, 28-49, speaks of 'the great schism' that tears apart the people of God and yet 'presupposes an over-arching common element' (29); cf. also his *When the Gods are Silent* (see n. 1 to Chapter I), 164-169. In his essay, 'Kontinuität und Diskontinuität des Volkes Gottes,' in *Das gespaltene Gottesvolk*, 267-282, G. Harder discusses this question competently but unlike K.H. Miskotte, *Das Judentum als Frage*, 116, 166ff., he still operates with contrasts such as law-gospel, cult-sacrament, unbelief-faith. Harder understands the Gospel of Matthew to say that the 'old people of God' is replaced by the new, so much so that 'a sharp division' between the church and 'the former Israel' exists.
48. Rat der Evang. Kirche in Deutschland, *Christen und Juden* (see n. 1 to Introduction), 21.
49. *Orientation* VII bc.
50. *The Church in the Power of the Spirit*, 148.
51. *Theologie des Paulus*, 284.
52. This explains why in 1970 K.H. Miskotte published essays under the title *Das Judentum als Frage an die Kirche* (see n. 1 to Introduction). Among the questions which Judaism asks of *all the world* are the following: According to the structure of Greek thought and life, the cosmos is a unified whole,

constituted and firm in itself—but is this cosmos the core of reality? Events, processes, and evolution in the realm of nature are being deified—but does the fertility of the earth deserve this idolisation? The *status quo* is worshipped and an *amor fati* helps to bear adversities—but is there another meaning of life except the realisation of that which is good (7-8)?

Questions posed by Judaism *to Christianity* in particular are: Are you Christians really praying for the coming of God's kingdom, in a manner that engages your own selves—or are you doing no more than comforting and placating your souls? Who has entitled you to consider our Jewish religion a preparation for your Christendom, to declare your 'ethical Messianism' superior to our Messianic hope? What right do you have to engage yourselves in a 'mission to the Jews'? Do you really believe in redemption—or is your 'faith' no more than an instrument to come to terms with the present status of the world? Are you pleased by the fact that we Jews are hated and persecuted for the sake of God who is one, while you have settled safely in the world? Are you still waiting for the Messiah (9-16)? Cf. also *When the Gods are Silent*, 309-315.

53.   More than once, this question has been raised in discussions within the World Council of Churches. It is mentioned also in the document of the Dutch Hervormde Kerk, *Israel und die Kirche*, 43, 52-53, and n. 19. See also the quotations collected below, in Part I n. 57; Part III nn. 114 and 117. R. Rendtorff, 'Der Staat Israel und die Christen,' in *Christlich-jüdisches Forum* 47, Basel, 1975, 1-14, 9, appears not to be aware of the urgency of this issue when he declares that an affirmative answer 'is a very remote notion.' Indeed, it appears hardly possible ever to find authorised spokesmen for *all* Jews; but this difficulty must not smother all attempts to include Jews in ecumenical deliberations. At present, Jews and Arabic Christians only seldom meet in Geneva and elsewhere under the auspices of the WCC. Their very meeting together, even when it fails to produce more than a first (superficial) mutual acquaintance, may eventually contribute to the destruction of hate-images fostered on both sides, and to the reduction of existing tensions.

54.   Although Tertullian, *De Pudicitia* 8-9, fought this exposition of the parable, it was represented in the ancient church by, among others, Jerome (Migne, *Patrologia Latina* XXX, 574-575), and it is taken up again by J.D.M. Derrett, 'The Parable of the Prodigal Son,' *NTS* 14 (1967), 56-74; repr. in *Law in the New Testament*, London: Darton, Longman & Todd, 1970, 100-125.

55.   An analogy may be found in the permanent dialectic between being and act, static and dynamic, institutional establishment and charismatic freedom, as it has been proposed for intra-mural church use by J.-L. Leuba, *Institution et Evènement*, Neuchâtel/Paris: Delachaux & Niestlé, 1950.

56.   J. Moltmann, *The Church in the Power of the Spirit*, 147-148, has chosen the first three petitions of the Lord's Prayer in order to illustrate this. Studies on the Jewish roots of, and parallels to, the Lord's Prayer such as H.L. Strack

and P. Billerbeck, *Kommentar zum Neuen Testament aus Talmud und Midrasch*, I (1922), 406-423; E. Lohmeyer, *The Lord's Prayer*, London: Collins, 1965; K.G. Kuhn, *Achtzehngebet und Vaterunser und der Reim*, WUNT I (1950); J. Jeremias, *The Lord's Prayer*, Philadelphia: Fortress, 1964, reveal that *all* petitions draw from a common root.

57. G. Eichholz, *Theologie des Paulus*, 288-292, 300 affirms, 'A Gentile [-Christian] church that would write off Israel, the people not written off by God, is in danger of writing off herself.' K. Kupisch, 'Nach Auschwitz' (see n. 45), 286, says, 'The church needs the continuous presence of Israel'; and K.E. Skydsgaard, 'Israel, Kirche und die Einheit des Gottesvolkes,' in *Das gespaltene Gottesvolk* (see n. 45), 294-297, concludes his essay with the words, 'The church cannot dispense with Israel, and Israel cannot do without the church.' F. Rosenzweig, *The Star of Redemption*, 413, makes the same point: 'If the Christian did not have the Jew at his back he would lose his way wherever he was.'

58. The 'occasionalistic' understanding of the church, attributed to K. Barth (and criticised) by J. Hamer, *Karl Barth*, Paris: Desclée de Brouwer, 1949, 137ff., does not correspond to the biblical witness. For by the revelation and word of God a people was created and is sustained which (though not by a prolongation of the incarnation of the Word, nor by unchangeable dogmas nor institutions, but by God's faithfulness) is subordinated to the Jew Jesus and connected with the history of all Jews. By this subordination and connection the church is constituted and granted indestructible continuity. F.-W. Marquardt, in his book on the rediscovery of Israel (see n. 1 to Introduction) has shown that this insight is a decisive feature of K. Barth's theology.

59. *Orientation* VII b.

NOTES TO CHAPTER TWO

1. See the documents prepared for the Consultation between officials of the World Council of Churches and of the (now defunct) Near Eastern Bureau of Information and Interpretation, held in Beirut in the autumn of 1972. These documents are available in mimeographed form at the WCC, 150 route de Ferney, CH-1211 Geneva 20. Similar voices are heard in Eastern theological responses to the French Bishops' *Orientation*, to which reference was made in n.21 to Chapter I.

2. With increasing zeal and passion questions such as the following are asked and answered in divergent ways: Are the chapters Rom. 9-11 the substance of an original, independent tractate, or are they a necessary logical link in the structure of the whole of Romans because they include indispensable information on grace, on the history of salvation and of the world, on election, on justification, or on the unity in Christ? Does Paul, in this section of Romans, address himself only to Gentile-Christians, or does he at the same

time also intend to be heard and heeded by Judaeo-Christians and by unbaptised Jews? Are the strong and the weak described in Rom. 14-15 Gentile- and Judaeo-Christians respectively? Neither these problems nor the issues of election, remnant, mystery, and other individual difficulties will be discussed in detail in the following.

3.   Because in Rom. 11:26 'all Israel' and in 9:27 and 11:1-7 the 'remnant' of Israel is mentioned, it is most likely that the origin of Paul from Benjamin has symbolic significance for the apostle. When after Solomon's death the Northern and the Southern Kingdoms ('Israel' and 'Judah') formed separate political entities, only the tribe of Benjamin joined the tribe of Judah in order to remain faithful to the house of David (I Kgs. 12:21; in I Kings 11:31-32, 35-36, and elsewhere, however, only the tribe of Judah is described as loyal to David's offspring). If the note of I Kings 12:21 is reliable, then at the time of the divided realms (according to Jeremiah, also after the destruction of the Northern Kingdom), Benjamin is the quasi-representative ambassador of the Northern Kingdom, that is, of the whole of Israel, within the Kingdom of Judah. Thus it is probable that Paul, a Benjamite, considered himself a citizen who, while belonging to Judah, was also representative of 'all Israel.' In turn (and primarily in those passages in the books of Joshua, Samuel, and Kings that show traces of 'deuteronomistic redaction'), the term 'all Israel' often signifies the united northern and southern tribes; cf. nn. 6 and 11. Further, in later Old Testament books 'all Israel' signifies all the Jews who returned from Babylon, particularly the members of the former Southern Kingdom who were reunited in the promised land (Ezr. 2:70; 6:16-17; 10:5).

4.   So e.g. E. Käsemann, *Commentary on Romans*, London: SCM, 1980, 253-318; *idem*, 'Paul and Israel,' 194-197. K. Stendahl, however, in his Foreword to J. Munck, *Christ and Israel*, Philadelphia: Fortress Press, 1967, viii, insists that Rom. 9-11 are not a tractate—be it on 'the interesting theological idea of predestination' or on 'justification by faith.'

5.   An entirely different judgment is passed on the significance of the Old Testament by, for example, P. Vielhauer, 'Paulus und das Alte Testament,' in L. Abramowski and J.F.G. Goeters (eds.), *Studien zur Geschichte und Theologie der Reformation. Festschrift E. Bizer*, Neukirchen: Neukirchener Verlag, 1969, 33-62; *Geschichte der urchristlichen Literatur*, Berlin/New York: de Gruyter, 1975, 770-780. According to Vielhauer, in the proclamation of the gospel of Jesus Christ the Holy Scriptures of the Old Testament fulfilled no more than a 'secondary and subsidiary' function; they served 'as an apologetic and polemical instrument to interpret what God had done in Christ, yet not as a critical norm.' Against this opinion speak the similarity *and* the differences between Pauline hermeneutics and the use of the Scriptures made in Qumran, by the apocalyptic literature, and in the Mishnah. L. Baeck, 'The Faith of Paul' (see n. 35 to Chapter 1), 109, has a better conception of Paul's intention: 'Paul was a theologian . . . not incidentally . . . by his nationality. As a Jew, his life was contained in the Bible, and as a Jewish scholar he had to justify before

the Bible whatever he would say or do'; he had to lay bare the meaning of the biblical words, for without biblical interpretation his proclamation could not be legitimate.

6.   In the opening of Rom. 11:25 reference is made to a μυστήριον (mystery, secret). The use of this term may be a signal, saying that the three affirmations made in Rom. 11:25b-26a (a part of Israel was hardened; this happened until the fulness of the nations should come in; this way all Israel will be saved) were found by Paul in a (now lost) prophetic-apocalyptic book, or that they stem from a New Testament prophet. What such a book or prophet had said about the fulfilment of Hosea's, Jeremiah's, and Ezekiel's prophecies regarding the reunion of the twelve tribes in *one* people would then be quoted by Paul—just as in other cases he quotes not only the Scriptures (see e.g. I Cor. 2:9; 14:34; 15:45; Rom. 2:20; Gal. 2:16; Eph. 5:14). If the citation is taken from a Jewish rather than from a Christian source, the term 'all Israel' might have included no more than all *proselytes* from the nations, not necessarily all nations. Cf. n. 11.

7.   For instance, E. Käsemann, *Commentary on Romans*, 253ff., 241ff.; A. Schlatter, *Gottes Gerechtigkeit*, Stuttgart: Calwer Vereinsbuchhandlung, 1935, 291ff.; A. Nygren, *Commentary on Romans*, London: SCM Press, 1952, 353ff.; E. Gaugler, *Der Römerbrief*, II, Zurich: Zwingli-Verlag, 1952, 3ff.; C.K. Barrett, *A Commentary on the Epistle to the Romans*, London: A. & C. Black, 1957, 174ff.; J. Huby, *Saint Paul, Épître aux Romains*, Paris: Beauchesne, 1957, 320ff. Agreement prevails particularly in the titles given to part II: it is understood as a reproach of Israel. In deviating from the consensus regarding part III, A. Schlatter gives Rom. 11 the title, 'The Work of Grace in Judaism.' The concord regarding Part II is most drastically broken by K. Barth, *Church Dogmatics* II (1957), 213-233, 240-259, 267-305: in his interpretation of each of the three parts, the inclusion in God's election and grace not only of the remnnant of Israel, but even of that (part of) Israel which rejects the gospel of Jesus Christ, is explicitly affirmed. This exposition implies a *character indelebilis* conferred upon Israel. U. Luz, *Das Geschichtsverständnis des Paulus*, Munich: Kaiser, 1968, also makes steps towards a christological interpretation of these chapters.

8.   In Gal. 4:21-31, Isaac and Ishmael, the spiritual and the fleshly son, are juxtaposed in corresponding fashion.

9.   Analogous is the inclusion of the 'rebel' in the community worshipping God through the celebration of the Seder (the Passover Feast), up to the present time. Among the four children sitting at the table and asking ritual questions, one is rebellious. He receives a sharp reply, but he is not thrown out.

10.   Cf. Rom. 9:13; 11:8-10; Is. 6:9-10; Acts 28:26-28; Matt. 13:14-15; Job 12:38-40.

11.   These Pauline interpretations are rather surprising. But since they are probably influenced by rabbinical exposition of the Scripture, they should not be called arbitrary. For instance, according to some rabbis, Is. 57:19 (the verse

announcing peace to those far and near) was interpreted as referring to the admission of proselytes to God's people; see the references in Strack-Billerbeck, III, 585-586. This rabbinical exposition takes up a tradition traceable already in (the Deuteronomistic) parts of the Old Testament. When, under the influence of Judaean (southern) prophets, the origin of the Northern Kingdom is described in the two books of Kings, much emphasis is given to the introduction of worshipping the calf, among the tribes that had defected from the house of David; the infidel Israelites are shown to have chosen the way of heathens, that is, of idol-makers and idol-worshippers. In II Kings 17:24-41 it is reported that after the destruction of Samaria in 722/21 B.C., the population of the former Northern Kingdom was mixed with Gentile elements. Ezek. 37 (probably composed of pieces that originally were conceived independently of one another) in its present composition and shape illustrates the meaning of resurrection from the dead. The resuscitation seen in a vision (Ezek. 37:1-14; cf. Rom. 11:15) signifies two seemingly different events: the reunion of the Northern and Southern Kingdoms under *one* king and around *one* sanctuary, *and* the spread of the knowledge of God among the nations (Ezek. 37:15-28). Similarly, in the Gospel of John (4:4-42; 10:16), the Samaritan woman represents the sheep of Jesus chosen *not* from the Judaean (or Jewish?) sheepfold and yet belonging in the flock tended by the *one* shepherd. It is the Samaritans, who, to our surprise, confess that Jesus is the 'Saviour of the World,' and not just of Judaea or of Israel.

12.   Rom. 4:25; Gal. 3:13; II Cor. 5:21.

13.   Indeed, Calvin, *Institutes*, III 22:1; 24:5; and, *De aeterna Dei praedestinatione, Corpus Reformatorum, Calvini Opera*, VIII 306, 318, called Jesus Christ 'the mirror of election' (*electionis speculum*). But only by P. Maury, 'Election et foi' (1936), repr. in *Foi et Vie* 54 (1956), 199-219; German tr. 'Erwählung und Glaube,' *Theol. Stud.* 8 (1940), and (following him) by K. Barth, 'Gottes Gnadenwahl,' *Theologische Existenz heute* 47 (1936), was a new conception of 'double predestination' developed. What in the Reformed orthodoxy of the centuries after the Reformation resembled fatalistic determinism was now shown to be based on the historic tension and unity of Christ's cross and resurrection. The way from Calvary to Easter was shown to be the heart of the mystery of election and reprobation: even the rejected son was elected, in the end. In K. Barth's doctrine on double predestination contained in his *Church Dogmatics* II/2, 3-506, the theological co-inherence of the three pairs is constitutive: (i) Christ's cross and resurrection; (ii) the history of Israel and the church; and (iii) reprobation and election.

14.   J. Munck, *Christ and Israel*, 79, uses the words 'The unbelief of the Jews toward Christ during his life on earth' as a subtitle *only* to Rom. 9:30-10:4, i.e., the first subsection of Part II. But in his comments on the central and main subsection of Rom. 10, that is, of vv. 5-13, he writes on p. 84, 'Paul is not trying in this passage to point out and prove the guilt of the Jews, but . . . throughout chapter 10 his aim is to show that God has done everything to win the Jews for the faith.' He makes similar statements on pp. 89-90 about Rom. 10:14-21.

Under the subtitle, 'God has done everything in order that the Jews may believe and call upon Christ,' he asserts, 'It is surprising that commentators are almost unanimous in agreeing that the aim of chapter 10, including 10:14-21, is to demonstrate Israel's guilt ... Of course, Israel's guilt is actually mentioned but it is not stressed as a main theme.' See the similar affirmation of U. Luz, *Das Geschichtsverständnis des Paulus*, 1968, 30. K. Barth, *A Shorter Commentary on Romans*, London: SCM Press, 1959, 112, speaks of the 'human recalcitrance even against the grace of God which was manifested in Jesus Christ.' C.E.B. Cranfield, *The Epistle to the Romans*, II, ICC, 1979, 503, affirms that 'a hopeful note ... focusses attention not on Israel's sin but on God's goodness toward Israel.'

15. Compare the reference to the obedience of Jesus Christ and the fulfilment of the Law in him, in Rom. 5:19; Phil. 2:8; Gal. 2:20; 3:13.

16. See R. Bring, *Commentary on Galatians*, Philadelphia: Muhlenberg, 1961, 128-142, and C.E.B. Cranfield, 'St. Paul and the Law,' *SJT* 17 (1964), 43-68, esp. 49ff.

17. Cf. I Cor. 1:18-24; 2:8; Gal. 5:11; I Thess. 2:15-16.

18. Cf. Deut. 5:26; 8:3; 30:6, 15, 19-20; 32:47; etc. Is it necessary to conclude that because Paul presents a christological interpretation of the Law (called 'word') in Deut. 30:14, he therefore intended to teach his readers that among Christians Christ has taken that place which the Law occupies among Jews? Hardly, for just as Jesus says that he came to fulfil not to destroy the Law (according to Matt. 5:17-20), so for Paul Christ is the fulfilment of the Law by faith and love. Thus, following Paul, Christ establishes the Law and does not invalidate it. 'Do we then overthrow the law by this faith? By no means! On the contrary, we uphold the law' (Rom. 3:31).

19. Is. 42:6; Gen. 12:1-3; Ex. 19:6; Jonah *passim*.

20. In Rom. 9:31-32 Paul describes Jews as 'not succeeding' in fulfilling the Law, as 'falling over the stumbling stone,' and in Rom. 11:11-12 he speaks of their fall, trespass, and failure. R. Bultmann's reference to their *Scheitern* ('shattering'; the German term means originally 'being shipwrecked'; in 'Prophecy and Fulfillment,' 206-207, the terms 'come to grief' and 'miscarriage' are employed by the translator) may have some support in Luke 20:18: 'every one who falls on that stone will be broken to pieces; but when it falls on any one it will crush him.' But Paul does not have in mind a catastrophe that kills but rather a failure to attain a given goal. According to Phil. 3:4-8, he himself had indeed written off as a 'loss' all of what he was proud of in earlier years; he calls it 'manure.' At that time, he considered himself 'in legal rectitude, faultless,' not shattered or crushed.

21. It appears necessary to draw the conclusion that only Jesus Christ in person is the remnant of Israel. Indeed, in Rom. 9:27-28, 'seed' and 'remnant' are used as synonyms, and in a clever exegetical step Paul does not interpret 'seed of Abraham' in a collective sense in Gal. 3:16, but as a designation of the Messiah to come. However, in Rom. 11:1-7, he does not explicitly call Christ

'*the* remnant' or '*the* seed.'

22.   It is not only unknown, but highly questionable, too, whether Paul ever urged Jews (e.g., when addressing the Sanhedrin or people assembled in synagogues) to become jealous of the baptised Gentiles. Even more dubious is the presumed right of the church, especially its Gentile-Christian majority members, to encourage Jews to do so. To my knowledge, there is only one single instance of a Pauline speech in which such a motivation on the part of a Jew for conversion to faith in Jesus Christ is touched upon: in Gal. 2:15-16 Paul reminds Peter that 'we sinners of Jewish extraction' (such as Paul and Peter) 'even we, too, began to believe in the Messiah Jesus' because we 'had come to know that a person is not justified by works of law, but through the faith of the Messiah Jesus.' The 'person' (ἄνθρωπος) here mentioned may not be a dogmatical construct, that is, an abstraction or generalisation, but rather Adam (Rom. 5:12-21), or Abraham before his circumcision (Rom. 4:3-22, esp. 10-12), or persons such as Cornelius, the centurion of Caesarea (Acts 10-11). The use of the phrase 'we too' in Gal. 2:16 may indeed imply something like jealousy regarding the justification of Gentiles by grace which had contributed to the conversion of Paul and Peter.

23.   See esp. Is. 2:2-4; Mic. 4:1-4; Is. 60:5-16; 66:19-20; Hagg. 2:7-9; Zech. 14:16-19.

24.   This interpretation of the collection for Jerusalem is found in chapter 10 of J. Munck, *Paul and the Salvation of Mankind*, 1959.

25.   In Acts 23:6; 24:15; 26:6-7; 28:20; cf. Eph. 1:12; 4:9, reference is made to the oneness and sameness of the hope of Jews and Christians. At the meeting of the World Council of Churches at Evanston 1954, a declaration pointing out this particular identity was not adopted. See the 'Statement on the Hope of Israel,' *The Evanston Report, 1954*, London: SCM Press, 1955, 327-328.

26.   The statement made in Gal. 4:24, that 'these things are said allegorically' (literal translation), does not prove that in the following words Paul proposes what today is called an *allegorical* interpretation. Because in 4:29 Paul argues, 'just as then . . . so also now,' Gal. 4:21-31 ought rather to be called a *typological* exposition, as indeed is offered in, for example, I Cor. 10:6, 11; Rom. 5:14. In an allegory the literal sense and the historical events evaporate in favour of their spiritual meanings. In typology, however, a correspondence is stated between earlier and later events on the level of history (cf. R.P.C. Hanson, *Allegory and Event*, London: SCM, 1959, 7).

27.   Though literary and historical criteria fail to prove beyond any doubt that Galatians was written before Romans, biographical arguments and the probable development of Paul's doctrine favour the dating of Galatians before Romans. Cf. C.H. Buck, 'The Date of Galatians,' *JBL* 70 (1951), 113-127; C.E. Faw, 'The Anomaly of Galatians,' *Biblical Research* 4 (Chicago, 1960), 25-38; R. Jewett, *Paul's Anthropological Terms*, Leiden: Brill, 1971, 11-48; P. Feine, J. Behm, W.G. Kümmel, *Introduction to the New Testament*, London: SCM Press, 1965, 197-198.

28. Esp. in Eph. 1:12-13; 2:1-3, 11-22; 3:6. In what follows we agree with A. Harnack, E. Haupt, T.K. Abbott, B.F. Westcott, T. Zahn, J.A.T. Robinson, E. Percy, J. Schmid, R.M. Grant, A. Robert, A. Feuillet, and H. Schlier, in considering Ephesians authentic. Arguments for this position are collected in M. Barth, *Ephesians*, I, New York: Doubleday, Anchor Bible 34, 1974, 36-50; for detailed questions see the Index in *Ephesians*, II, 848, *s.v.* 'author.' M. Rese, 'Die Vorzüge Israels nach Röm. 9, 4f. und Eph. 2, 12,' *TZ* 31 (1975), 211-222, makes contradictory utterances on Ephesians. He is certainly right in observing that Ephesians says nothing on the hardening and the excision of Israel, nor on a remnant of this people. On the other hand, he argues that this letter cannot have been written by Paul because, according to its message and unlike the substance of the genuine Pauline writings, the particularity of Israel has moved to the church (220, 222). Though this proposition fits the above-mentioned theory of substitution (which claims support not only from passages such as I Pet. 2:4-10, but also from many uncontested Pauline statements), it is not substantiated by Ephesians; see especially Eph. 3:6.

29. It is hard to decide whether this verse speaks of the proclamation of Jesus Christ, made either between his baptism and his death, or immediately after his resurrection. It is also possible that the world-wide, apostolic proclamation of the name of Christ is in mind. For the way in which Paul handles the text of Is. 57:19, see above, n. 11.

30. Eph. 5:25-27; 1:22-23; 4:12, 16; 5:23, 30.

31. Eph. 2:7; 3:1-13, esp. 10; 6:18-29; cf. Col. 1:5-6, 23-29.

32. Regarding Eph. 4:13, see M. Barth, 'Die Parousie im Epheserbrief,' in H. Baltensweiler und Bo Reicke (eds.), *Neues Testament und Geschichte* (Festschrift O. Cullmann), Zürich: Theologischer Verlag, 1972, 238-250.

33. This is the title of an important book by J. Meuzelaar, Assen: van Gorcum, 1961. The substitution of 'one body *in* Christ' (Rom. 10:5) by 'the body of Christ' appears already in I Cor. 12:27.

34. J. Moltmann's work on the church bears this subtitle.

NOTES TO CHAPTER THREE

1. John 5:31, 34, 41; 7:17, in the NEB version. Concerning the 'variants' among Jesus' statements on his own witness, see e.g. R. Bultmann, *The Gospel of John*, Oxford: Blackwell, 1971, 278-281, and E.D. Freed, 'Variations in the Language and Thought of John,' *ZNW* 55 (1964), 167-197.

2. Except in his self-confession before the high priest (Mark 14:62) and the Samaritan woman (John 4:25-26), Jesus never explicitly called himself the Messiah.

3. Calvin, *Institutes*, I/6:2.

4. According to the evidence given by the New Testament the earliest Christians never used the title 'Christians' as a self-designation. They were

labelled that way—be it in mockery or with serious intentions—because a connection or resemblance between them and the Lord whose name they confessed must have impressed other persons; see Acts 11:26; I Pet. 4:16.

5.   Examples are the evaluation of Judaism (as a primitive tribal religion) in Hegel's philosophy of religion, the corresponding Tübingen image of the mutually exclusive relationship between Jewish and Gentile Christianity, and finally R. Bultmann's and E. Käsemann's reference to the shattering of Israel and the rejection of pious Jews. Such statements have nothing to do with a scholarly description of observed events, but they have the double effect of insult against the Jews and commiseration with those offended.

6.   What Paul says of himself in I Cor. 4:3, 5 applies also to Jews and Christians: 'If I am called to account by your or by any human court of judgment, it does not matter to me in the least . . . So pass no premature judgment; wait until the Lord comes. For he will bring to light what darkness hides' (NEB).

7.   In I Thess. 2:14-16 and elsewhere, Paul does not speak of heresy. Yet in Rom. 9:30-10:3 (cf. Phil. 3:9) he appears to condemn Israel as a whole as if the entire people stood on a level with a heresy found among Christians; cf. n. 9. As early as in Ignatius, *Phil.* VI 1; *Magn.* X 3, the combination of 'Judaism' and 'Christendom' is regarded as an absurdity; there is, he is convinced, only a one-way street: out of Judaism into Christendom! Since the times of Irenaeus, *Adv. Haer.* I 26:1-2, and Chrysostom, *Adv. Judaeos, Gentiles et Haereticos* (Migne, PG XLVIII, 1075-1080; cf. 813-838) and Augustine, *Adv. Judaeos, Paganos et Arianos* (Migne, PL XXXXII = Augustinus VIII, 1116-1130) 'the Jews' have their place among the worst pagan company. Surveys on the history and the methods of anti-Jewish polemics are given in the works mentioned at the end of n. 20 to Chapter I.

8.   As shown by C. Klein, *Anti-Judaism in Christian Theology*, London: SPCK, 1978, there are wilful distortions and caricatures which have nothing to do with scholarly procedures. If the anti-Judaism of Christian authors was an instigator rather than only a victim of pagan anti-Semitism, Christians certainly have reason to blush with shame.

9.   The generalisation regarding the attitude and acts of the Jews (or of the Jewish authorities in Jerusalem and in the diaspora?) which is obviously made in I Thess. 2:14-16 may be due to the impact of acute persecutions—though M. Dibelius, *An die Thessalonicher*, Tübingen: Mohr, 1937, 11-12, denies it. Paul attributes to the whole of 'Israel' the attempt to attain to salvation by means of works and human righteousness. Paul himself had been an exemplary Jew in his endeavour to live up to the 'traditions of the Fathers,' and he had put himself into the service of the authorities which arranged for the persecutions of Christians (Gal. 1:13-14, 23; I Cor. 15:9; Phil. 3:3-6; Acts 8:1, 3; 9:1-2, 21; etc.). Perhaps Paul drew conclusions from his own attitude towards Christians and could at times even think that all Jews were like himself. Paul disrupts his own generalisation when in Rom. 11:1-7 he speaks of a proto-

typical 'remnant' of Israel (Elijah and the seven thousand faithful) who reached the goal of righteousness by grace, not through works, and without being shattered by the Law. Cf. n. 20 to Chapter II. John's Gospel contains passages which seem to generalise as readily as does Paul on certain occasions. Still, the Fourth Gospel also speaks of a 'schism' among the Jewish people, caused by the fact that 'many Jews' believed in Jesus Christ.

10.   So for instance L. Baeck und M. Buber, in ever new forms.

11.   K.H. Miskotte, *Het Wezen der Joodse Religie* (2nd ed. 1962), carefully presents and discusses a series of Jewish portrayals of Jewish faith and life. Miskotte first published this description of the works of scholars and poets of the late nineteenth and the twentieth centuries before the State of Israel was founded (the undated 1st edition was published in 1937). His book calls urgently for complementation which would start with Abraham (viz. with the earliest Hebrew songs and writers such as the Yahwist) or with the Exile, and which, after a description of hellenistic, talmudic, medieval, hassidic, assimilatory Judaism, would lead up to the religious and the secular features of present-day Zionism.

12.   The document of the Evangelische Kirche in Deutschland, 'Christen und Juden,' 34, reveals dissatisfaction with the concept 'dialogue with Israel' which for the past twenty or thirty years seemed to provide all that was necessary. Without much costlier investment of effort progress will scarcely be made in the search for the unity of God's people.

13.   According to *Nostra Aetate* V, the relationship between Christians and Jews is merely a part or example of the brotherly attitude which Christians owe to all mankind. The title of *Nostra Aetate* ('Declaration on the Relation of the Church to the Non-Christian Religions') subordinates Judaism to the many 'non-Christian religions.' Thus the fact is obfuscated, if not negated, that the Jews are the older brother of the Christians, without whom the junior would have neither his place nor his particular role in God's house. The statement, 'salvation is from the Jews,' cannot be simply enlarged by the words, ' . . . and also from a decent attitude to other nations and religions.'

14.   The substance of these sentences is almost literally drawn from several parts of K.E. Skydsgaard, 'Israel, die Kirche und die Einheit des Gottesvolkes,' in *Das gespaltene Gottesvolk* (see n. 45 to Chapter 1), 294-297.

15.   See, for instance, H.J. Schoeps, *Paul*, 120-121, 124, 139, 149, 256-257.

16.   Cf. John 1:17; 3:21; 5:33; etc. In Paul's writings, especially in Rom. 1-3, 'truth' is almost a synonym of 'righteousness.'

17.   See n. 22 for utterances on the continuous threat to the church by the pagan patrimony which Gentile-Christians have brought into the church. The Dutch Hervormde Kerk, in *Israel und die Kirche* (1961), 53, speaks of that menace.

18.   There is an often ignored predecessor to the labours of the World Council of Churches and the Vatican Secretariat for Unity: the so-called 'Mercersburg Theology,' developed in the USA in the middle of the 19th

century. See J.H. Nichols, *Romanticism in American Theology*, Chicago: University of Chicago Press, 1961, and *The Mercersburg Theology*, New York: Library of Protestant Thought, 1966.
19.   In *Das gespaltene Gottesvolk* (see n. 45 to Chapter 1), 299, H. Grolle poses the question, 'What is ecumenism if we include in it the first schism— the schism existing in God's people, Israel, herself?' Among the responses given are the following: 'That which is God's truth we, the Catholics and Protestants, shall get to hear by no other means than by unflinchingly open dialogue with Israel' (W. Dantine, 169). 'Without Israel's participation, the dialogue between Christians of diverse churches and creeds will shatter' (W. Eckert, OP, 170). 'The church is in need of the continuous presence of Israel' (K. Kupisch, 286). 'The result for Israel is this: she has a decisive role to play in the dialogue about the re-union of Christians' (B. Lampert, OP, 290). Before Vatican Council II, K. Barth affirmed, 'The modern ecumenical movement suffers more seriously from the absence of Israel than of Rome or Moscow' (*Church Dogmatics* IV/3:2, 878). The titles of a Jewish and a Roman Catholic book confirm the impression that similar thoughts are fostered not only among Protestants: P.E. Lapide, *Ökumene aus Christen und Juden*, Neukirchen: Neukirchener Verlag, 1972, and C.T. Thoma (ed.), *Judentum und Kirche: Volk Gottes*, Zürich, Einsiedeln Köln: Benzinger, 1974. The Dutch Hervormde Kerk, *Israel und die Kirche*, 43, 52-53, points in the same direction, saying, 'Without Israel, the church cannot experience in full extent her ecumenical character ... For the encounter of the church with Israel, ecumenical unity means as much as the question, "To be or not to be?".' Without the inclusion of Israel—for the benefit of Christians, not in order to impose missionary pressure upon Jews!—there is no ecumenical unity of the churches.
20.   A report and documentation on the International Congress for World-Evangelism (July 16-25, 1974, in Lausanne, Switzerland) was published under the title, *Let the Earth Hear His Voice* I-II, Minneapolis: Worldwide Publications, 1974. At the beginning of Vol. I, the Lausanne Covenant is printed, which by its conciliatory tone surprised those who had anticipated violent outbursts against the World Council of Churches.
21.   *Breaking Barriers*, Nairobi 1975, ed. D.M. Paton, London: SPCK, 1975, 77, 162-165.
22.   Without explicit reference to organised ecumenical work, R. Niebuhr, 'The Relation of Christians and Jews in Western Civilization,' *Central Conference of American Rabbis Journal*, April 1958, 18-32; and in *The Godly and the Ungodly*, London: Faber and Faber, 1958, 86-112, esp. 108; and P. Tillich, 'The Theology of Missions,' *Christianity and Crisis* 15 (1955/56), 35-38, esp. 38, col. 1, have made similar affirmations. Repeatedly K.H. Miskotte, *Das Judentum als Frage an die Kirche* (e.g. 15 and 33), speaks of that 'paganism which is still alive in the souls [of Christians]. To this paganism which can be escaped as little as can nature, and which deploys inescapable power in the

form of "the One," "the All." To this paganism, Israel's God alone, "the only One," has opposed himself in his revelation' (cf. n. 52 to Chapter I). One evidence of 'latent paganism' must be mentioned explicitly: the seemingly undefeatable anti-Semitism; see Dutch Hervormde Kerk, *Israel und die Kirche*, 47.

23. Quoted in the version offered by R.H. Charles, *The Apocrypha and Pseudepigrapha* II, Oxford: Clarendon, 1913, 702. In the *Mishnah* (ed. by H. Danby, Oxford: The University Press, 1933), 452, the reference is Pirke Aboth III: 16. Prof. Zwi Werblowski of the Hebrew University, Jerusalem, has drawn my attention to the fact that E. Urbach, *The Sages*, Jerusalem: Magnes Press, 1975, gives this passage a novel interpretation: reportedly it describes God watching man, rather than God's providence, and it is said to contain a polemic against Paul. So far Urbach's book has not been accessible to me. A close connection between determinism and full personal responsibility is certainly made in the rabbinical doctrine of the Two Inclinations (Sir. 15:1-20, esp. vv. 14-15; Midr. Bereshith 27, on Gen. 6:6; b. Kiddushin 30b). Cf. also Sir. 16:15-30; 23:20-21; 33:7-18; 39:17-21; Josephus, War, II 162-3; Ant., XIII 172; XVIII 12-14; Psalms of Solomon 5:1-21(18); 9:1-10; I Enoch 41:8; 98:4; II Baruch 15:5-8; 19:1-4; Assumption of Moses 12:4-13; and in the Qumran literature: 1 QH XV 12ff.; CD II 7-8; 1 QS III 13ff. The absence from Paul's writings of a proper 'doctrine' of predestination, but also of a real paradox between God's and man's (freedom of) action, is elaborated by B. Meyer, *Unter Gottes Heilsratschluss*, Würzburg: Echter, 1974; see the review by U. Luz, *TLZ* 101 (1976), 843-844.

24. In *Das gespaltene Gottesvolk*, 186-187, K. Kupisch throws a challenge at his readers when he speaks of an imminent exchange of roles caused by the foundation of the State of Israel and by the formation of independent churches on what were formerly 'mission-fields': Israel stops being a people in diaspora and settles down, while the churches have to shoulder the task of being God's people in dispersion.

25. For instance, H. Lietzmann, *An die Römer*, Tübingen: Mohr, 4th ed. 1933, 65-68, and W. Bousset, *Kyrios Christos*, Nashville: Abingdon, 1970, chap. 1, describe the transformation. The Benedictine scholar Odo Casel in *Die Liturgie als Mysterienfeier*, Ecclesia Orans 9, Freiburg: Herder, 1923; and in 'Glaube, Gnosis und Mysterium,' *Jahrbuch für Liturgiewissenschaft* 15 (1941), 155-305, considers this development an enrichment and hails it, just because it demonstrates the influence and victory of pagan thought. A more critical stance is taken by K. Barth, *Church Dogmatics* IV 4 (1969); and in *The Christian Life*, Edinburgh: T. & T. Clark, 1981, at the end of para. 74, on his doctrine on baptism. Cf. M. Barth, *Die Taufe—ein Sakrament?*, Zollikon: Evangelischer Verlag, 1951.

26. Part I, final paragraph.

27. Cf. n. 56 to Chapter 1.

28. R. Panikkar, 'Inter-religious Dialogue: Some Principles,' *Journal of*

Ecumenical Studies 12 (1975), 407-409.

29.   Long before the Exile, prophets criticised the origin and practices of the monarchy with biting words; see Judg. 8:22-27; 9:7-20; I Sam. 8:4-9; 12:6-17 and the writings of Amos, First Isaiah, Hosea, and Jeremiah. But beside these denouncements stand promises given to David in II Sam. 7, in the classical prophets, and in many Psalms (e.g. in Ps. 2; 45; 80; 89; 110; 132).

30.   At the time of Samuel, Israel *was* given a king. Down to the fall of Samaria and Jerusalem, the prophets, historiographers, and poets gave testimony to the mercy of God which continued to be shown not only to the house of David but also to the changing dynasties of the Northern Kingdom. Prophets and other men of God kept on working in the northern territory. Even after the Exile, a king of David's house is expected as Messiah to come, whether that coming takes place within the course of human events or at their end. The post-exilic community of Israel was at the same time a cultic and a political entity; for long periods it fought to the best of its capabilities against amalgamation with ever-changing heathen cultures.

31.   Just like the majority of Pharisees, the majority of Christians in the east and west were ready to tolerate or promote cooperation with political powers. Among many examples one might mention: the caesaro-papism of the Constantinian Era; Augustine's vision of the rehabilitation of the crumbling Roman Empire by the vitality of the church; the struggles for political predominance between Pope and emperors of the Middle Ages; the Reformers who relied on princes and civil magistrates; the successive alliances between throne and altar; the foundation of the Vatican 'church-state' in the nineteenth century and the Concordats between the Vatican and the fascist states; and finally the newly formed associations of Christians with Marxist socialists. There have been true and false prophets in the history not only of the Jews but also of the churches.

In Eph. 2:12 (cf. 2:6) and Phil. 3:20, Paul uses juridical-political terms to denote the civil rights of Christians in the commonwealth of Israel *and* in heaven. Indeed, according to I Peter and Hebrews, Christians are strangers and aliens among the Gentiles of their environment, and yet they have a political role: Paul calls them 'ambassadors of reconciliation' (II Cor. 5:18-20). We mentioned earlier that the concept ἐκκλησία, 'church,' has a clear-cut political dimension. The church is given binding, if not legal, norms and forms of individual and social conduct, directives and orders that are particular and yet still have analogies in secular ethics and institutions. For the church it is as impossible as for Judaism to restrict the righteousness, the freedom, and the peace given by God to the realm of the soul, of religion, or of the individual person only.

32.   The quoted formulations stem from W. Guggenheim, *30 mal Israel*, Zürich: Ex Libris Verlag, 1976, 28.

33.   *Ibid.*, 91.

34.   Koenig's 'Report' has not (yet) been officially published but reached the

press by indiscretion. Prime Minister J. Rabin chose to ignore it when he was challenged to take a position on it in the Knesset. A sketch of its contents is found in the *Newsweek* issue of Sept. 27, 1976.

35.   To quote the retired Israeli General Mattityahu Peled.

36.   According to the Torah, the promised land was given to Israel as an estate in fee, not as property, and Israel was enjoined to consider the same law as valid for both natives and strangers.

INDEXES

INDEX OF PASSAGE REFERENCES

Genesis

12:1-3	43, 61, 85
16:10-15	45
21:13-21	45
45:4	6

Exodus

4:23	61
19:6	61, 85
32:32	31

Leviticus

18:5	39

Deuteronomy

5:26	85
8:3	85
23:2-3	75
30:6, 15, 19-20	85
30:14	39
32:21	41
32:47	85

Joshua

24	12

Judges

8:22-27	92
9:7-20	92

I Samuel

8:4-9	92
12:6-17	92

II Samuel

7	92

I Kings

11:31-32, 35-36	82

I Kings

12:21	82

II Kings

17:24-41	84

I Chronicles

28:8	75

Nehemiah

13:1	75

Psalms

2	92
45	92
69:21-27	78
80	92
89:2-4, 28-37, 39	75, 92
109:1-19, 27-29	78
110	92
132	92
141:5	18

Proverbs

3:11-12	40
27:5-6	18

Isaiah

2:2-4	86
6:9-10	35, 76, 83
42:6	57, 61, 85
49:6, 8	57, 61
53	62
54	75
55	75
57:19	36, 83
60:5-16	86
65:1	41
66:19-20	86

Jeremiah

3	75
3:8	75
31:31	75, 76
32:38-41	75
33:20-26	75
35	75

Ezekiel

2:70	82
6:16-17	82
10:5	82
16:1-14	75
18	12
23	75
26	75
37	43, 84

Hosea

1	75
2	75
10:2	75

Micah

2:5	75
4:1-4	86

Haggai

2:7-9	86

Zechariah

11:14	75
14:16-19	86

Matthew

3:15	63
5:17-20	63, 85
8:11f.	15
13:16f.	76, 83
15:1-20	63

Matthew	
19:28	14
21:18f.	15
21:28-32	25
22:17f.	66
23:37	15
24:2	15
25:31-46	52
26:61	15
28:16-20	62

Mark	
6:52	76
14:62	87

Luke	
2:32	58
7:29	64
13:28	15
14:15-24	37
15:11ff.	25, 43
19:44	15
20:15-18	16, 85
22:32	63
23:24	76

John	
1:17	58, 89
3:21	89
4:4-42	84, 87
4:22	49
5:31, 34, 41	87
5:33	89
7:17	87
7:43	35
8:44	16
9:16	35
9:40	76
10:16	84
10:19	35
12:37-43	83
12:40	76
14:6	58

John	
19:11	66

Acts	
2:23	76
3:13-15	76
4:10	76
5:30	76
7	16
7:52	76
8:1, 3	88
9:1-2, 21	88
10	63, 86
10:39	76
11	63, 86
11:26	88
13:27-28	76
13:40-41	76
15:22	74
19:32, 39, 40	74
23:6	86
24:15	86
26:6-7	86
28:20	86
28:26-28	83

Romans	
1:17	19
2:5-16	52
2:17-29	40, 42, 77, 79
2:20	83
3:2-5	19, 29, 30, 52, 76
3:21-22	39
3:21-31	77, 85
4	13, 84, 86
5	13, 86
5:19	63, 85
6:3-11	38
8:3-4	63
8:14-19	12
8:29	38

Romans	
8:33	12
8:35-39	30
9-11	13-15, 23-24, 29-49, 52, 56, 59-61, 66, 74, 76-77, 79, 81-85, 88
9:6	17
9:25-26	11
10:4	21, 63
11:16ff.	12, 16, 20
12:1-2	12
13:1-7	66
14:10	52
15:7-12	31
15:10	74
16:25	38

I Corinthians	
1:2	74
1:18-24	85
2:4	53
2:7	38
2:8	18, 20, 76, 85
2:9	83
3:12-15	52
3:16	12
4:3-5	52, 88
5:7-8	12
6:19	12
7:19	14
10:1-13	12, 74, 86
10:18-21	12
11:24-26	12, 64
12	74
14	74
14:21	11
14:34	83
15	13

I Corinthians
15:9 — 88
15:12-18 — 38
15:45 — 83
19:9 — 74

II Corinthians
3 — 13, 17, 29, 45
3:1-3 — 52
3:4-18 — 12, 20, 76
4:7-12 — 38
5:10 — 52
5:18-20 — 92
5:21 — 40, 84
6:16 — 11
11:2 — 12

Galatians
1:12, 16 — 19
1:13-14 — 31, 74, 88
2 — 77
2:2 — 19
2:11-21 — 14, 15, 48, 85, 86
2:16 — 83
3 — 13
3:7, 29 — 12
3:13 — 40, 84, 85
3:16 — 85
3:23-4:7 — 75
3:26 — 12
3:28 — 14
4:21-31 — 12, 16, 17, 20, 45, 48, 77, 83, 86
5:1-12 — 77, 85
5:6 — 14
6:15-16 — 14

Ephesians
1:9-10 — 38, 47

Ephesians
1:12-14 — 20, 46, 47, 86
1:22-23 — 87
2 — 20, 29, 46, 47, 48, 75, 87
2:6 — 92
2:12 — 92
2:19 — 11
2:20-22 — 12, 45
2:11-22 — 14, 15, 29, 46, 47, 58
3:1-13 — 87
3:5-12 — 46
3:6 — 20, 29, 46, 48, 87
4 — 47, 87
4:9 — 86
4:17-19 — 20, 46, 76
4:21 — 19, 58
5 — 87
5:14 — 83
5:25-27 — 12, 47, 87
6 — 87

Philippians
2:5-11 — 38, 63, 85
3 — 13, 29
3:3 — 12
3:3-9 — 31, 77, 79, 85, 88
3:10, 21 — 38
3:20 — 11, 92

Colossians
1 — 87
1:27 — 38
2:8 — 63
3:12 — 12

1 Thessalonians
2:14-16 — 16, 18, 20,

1 Thessalonians
— 32, 48, 85, 88

II Timothy
2:10 — 12

Titus
1:1 — 12
2:14 — 11

Hebrews
8 — 45, 76
8:13 — 17
12:5-6 — 40
13:8 — 32

James
1:1 — 14
2:2 — 75

I Peter
2:4-10 — 11, 13, 75, 87
2:13-17 — 66
4:16 — 88

I John
5:6-8 — 63

Revelation
1:6 — 75
1:8, 17, 18 — 32
5:10 — 75
7:4ff. — 14
13 — 66
15 — 14
20:6 — 75
21:12 — 14
22:13 — 32

INDEX OF NAMES

Abbott, T.K. 87
Akiba 21
Althaus, P. 79
Aron, R. 76
Augustine 15, 54, 77, 88, 92
Baeck, L. 21, 25, 78, 82, 89
Bar Kochba 21
Barrett, C.K. 83
Barth, K. 73, 81, 83, 84, 85, 90, 91
Barth, M. 77, 87, 91
Baumgartner, W. see Köhler
Bea, A. Cardinal 73
Begin, M. 69
Ben Chorin, S. 22, 61, 76, 79
Ben Gurion, D. 68
Billerbeck, P.
    (Strack, H.L. and) 80,84
Bousset, W. 77, 91
Bowman, J. 76
Bring, R. 85
Buber, M. 21, 25, 68, 78, 89
Buck, C.H. 86
Bultmann, R. 15, 73, 76, 79, 85, 87, 88
Calvin, J. 51, 59, 76, 84, 87
Cerfaux, L. 78
Charles, R.H. 91
Chrysostom, J. 77, 88
Coppens, J. 78
Cranfield, C.E.B. 85
Dahl, N.A. 75
Dantine, W. 90
Davies, W.D. 73
Derrett, J.D.M. 80
Dibelius, M. 88
Eckert, W.P. 76, 90
Eichholz, G. 24, 26, 73, 79, 81
Faw, C.E. 86
Feine, P. 86
Feuillet, A. 87
Flusser, D. 76
Formstecher, S. 21, 78

Freed, E.D. 87
Fuller, R. 76
Gaugler, E. 83
Grässer, E. 76
Grant, R.M. 87
Grolle, H. 90
Guggenheim, W. 92
Ha-Levi, Yehuda 21, 78
Hamer, J. 81
Hanson, R.P.C. 86
Harder, G. 79
Harnack, A. von 77, 87
Haupt, E. 87
Hegel, F.G.W. 88
Hennecke, E. and
    Schneemelcher, W. 76
Herzl, T. 69
Huby, J. 83
Irenaeus 88
Isaac, J. 76
Jeremias, J. 81
Jerome 80
Jewett, R. 86
Ignatius 88
Jocz, J. 74
John XXIII, Pope 6
Käsemann, E. 15, 74, 76, 77, 82,
    83, 88
Klausner, J. 76, 78
Klein, Ch. 75
Klein, G. 88
Köhler, L. and
    Baumgartner, W. 75
Koenig, I. 70, 92
Kortzfleisch, S. von 77
Kraus, H.J. 74
Küng, H. 74
Kuhn, K.G. 81
Kupisch, K. 79, 81, 90, 91
Lampert, B. 90
Lapide, P.E. 76, 90

Leistner, R. 76
Lessing, G.E. von 52
Leuba, J.-L. 80
Levinson, I.M. 78
Lietzmann, H. 91
Lohmeyer, E. 81
Luther, M. 15
Luz, U. 83, 85, 91
Magnes, Y.L. 68
Maimonides 21, 78
Marcion 15, 18, 23
Marquardt, F.-W. 74, 81
Maury, P. 84
Mayer, R. 78
Meuzelaar, J. 87
Meyer, B. 91
Minear, P. 74
Miskotte, K.H. 49, 74, 75, 78, 79, 87, 89, 90
Moltmann, J. 24, 74, 77, 78, 79, 80
Müller, C. 74
Munck, J. 74, 84, 86
Mussner, F. 74
Nichols, J.H. 90
Niebuhr, R. 90
Nygren, A. 83
Oesterreicher, J.M. 77
Osten-Sacken, P. von der 76
Panikkar, R. 65, 91
Parkes, J.W. 74
Pelagius 54
Peled, M. 93
Percy, E. 87
Peterson, E. 74, 78
Philo 12, 75
Pius XI, Pope 6

Rabin, J. 93
Rendtorff, R. 80
Rengstorf, K.-H. 77
Rese, M. 87
Richardson, P. 74, 78
Ridderbos, H. 79
Robert, A. 87
Robinson, J.A.T. 76, 87
Rosenzweig, F. 21, 25, 78, 81
Rost, L. 75
Rubinstein, R. 22, 79
Schlatter, A. 83
Schlier, H. 87
Schmid, J. 87
Schmidt, K.L. 74
Schneemelcher, W. see Hennecke
Schoeps, H.J. 21, 22, 78, 79, 89
Schrage, W. 75, 79
Sandmel, S. 76
Skydsgaard, K.E. 81, 89
Stendahl, K. 82
Strack, H. L. see Billerbeck
Stuhlmacher, P. 74
Tertullian 80
Thomas, J. 75
Tillich, P. 61, 90
Torrance, T.F. 74
Urbach, E. 91
Vermes, G. 76
Vielhauer, P. 82
Westcott, B. F. 87
Whiteley, D.E.H. 78
Wilckens, U. 75, 77
Williams, A.L. 77
Zahn, T. 87

INDEX OF DOCUMENTS

Berlin-Weissensee (Evangelische Kirche in Deutschland = EKD) 73
Breaking Barriers (World Council of Churches = WCC, Nairobi 1975) 90
Christen und Juden (EKD 1975) 73, 79, 89
The Christian Approach to Jews (WCC, Amsterdam 1948) 73
Church Constitution (Dutch Hervormde Kerk = DHK 1951) 63, 73
The Church and the Jewish People (WCC 1967) 73
Consultation WCC and Near Eastern Bureau of Information (Beirut 1972) 81
Erklärung der deutschen Bischöfe (1980) 73
Israel and the Church (DHK 1961) 73, 80, 90, 91
Israel: People, Land and State (DHK 1970) 73
Let the Earth Hear his Voice (World Evangelism Conference 1974) 90
Nostra Aetate (Vatican II 1963) 24, 73, 77, 89
Orientation Pastorale (French Bishops 1972) 23, 24, 57, 71, 73, 77, 79, 81
Orientations et Suggestions (Vatican Secretariat for Unity 1975) 64, 73
Rheinische Synode (1980) 73
Statement on the Hope of Israel (WCC, Evanston 1954) 73, 86
Zagorsk Declaration (Christian Peace Conference 1967) 77

Also published by JSOT Press, Department of Biblical Studies, The University of Sheffield, Sheffield S10 2TN, England.

Journal for the Study of the New Testament (*JSNT*)
(began publication 1978)

JSNT Supplement Series

1 THE BARREN TEMPLE AND THE WITHERED TREE
William R. Telford

2 STUDIA BIBLICA 1978: II. PAPERS ON THE GOSPELS
Edited by E.A. Livingstone

3 STUDIA BIBLICA 1978: III. PAPERS ON PAUL AND OTHER NEW TESTAMENT AUTHORS
Edited by E.A. Livingstone

4 FOLLOWING JESUS: DISCIPLESHIP IN THE GOSPEL OF MARK
Ernest Best

Gospel Perspectives
Edited by R.T. France and D. Wenham

I STUDIES OF HISTORY AND TRADITION IN THE FOUR GOSPELS

II STUDIES OF HISTORY AND TRADITION IN THE FOUR GOSPELS

III STUDIES IN MIDRASH AND HISTORIOGRAPHY

Journal for the Study of the Old Testament (*JSOT*)
(began publication 1976)

JSOT Supplement Series
Recent titles include

12 THE JUST KING:
MONARCHICAL JUDICIAL AUTHORITY IN ANCIENT ISRAEL
Keith W. Whitelam

15 THE DEUTERONOMISTIC HISTORY
Martin Noth

16 PROPHECY AND ETHICS:
ISAIAH AND THE ETHICAL TRADITIONS OF ISRAEL
Eryl W. Davies

19 ART AND MEANING:
RHETORIC IN BIBLICAL LITERATURE
Edited by David J.A. Clines, David M. Gunn and Alan J. Hauser

23 THE GLORY OF ISRAEL:
THE THEOLOGY AND PROVENIENCE OF THE ISAIAH TARGUM
Bruce D. Chilton

25 THE DAMASCUS COVENANT:
AN INTERPRETATION OF THE 'DAMASCUS DOCUMENT'
Philip R. Davies

Catalogue and price list available from JSOT Press.

DATE DUE

HIGHSMITH 45-220